More Cotswolds

Walks

Compiled by
Brian Conduit

Fully revised by
Nick Channer

Acknowledgements
My thanks for the valuable advice and numerous useful leaflets that I
obtained from the various tourist information centres throughout the area.
Also I am grateful for the help given by the National Trust in planning Walk
23 through Sherborne Park.

Text: Brian Conduit
                    Revised text for 2009 edition, Nick Channer
Photography: Brian Conduit, Crimson Publishing and
                    Nick Channer
Editorial: Ark Creative (UK) Ltd
Design: Ark Creative (UK) Ltd

ISBN: 978-1-85458-542-4

While every care has been taken to ensure the accuracy
of the route directions, the publishers cannot accept responsibility for errors
or omissions, or for changes in details given. The countryside is not static:
hedges and fences can be removed, field boundaries can alter, footpaths can
be rerouted and changes in ownership can result in the closure or diversion of
some concessionary paths. Also, paths that are easy and pleasant for walking
in fine conditions may become slippery, muddy and difficult in wet weather,
while stepping stones across rivers and streams may become impassable.
    If you find an inaccuracy in either the text or maps, please write to
Crimson Publishing at the address below.

First published 2000 by Jarrold Publishing
Revised and reprinted 2006, 2009.

This edition first published in Great Britain 2009 by Crimson Publishing, a
division of:
Crimson Business Ltd,
Westminster House, Kew Road, Richmond, Surrey, TW9 2ND

Printed in Singapore. 4/09

A catalogue record for this book is available from the British library.

Front cover: Longborough
Previous page: Owlpen Manor, near Dursley, Gloucestershire

Contents

■ Short, easy walks

■ Walks of modest length, likely to involve some modest uphill walking

■ More challenging walks which may be longer and/or over more rugged terrain, often with some stiff climbs

Keymap 1

Pershore
EVESHAM
Broadway

Upton upon Severn
Tewkesbury
Bredon
Northway
Ashton under Hill
Winchcombe

Bishop's Cleeve
Cleeve Hill
Prestbury

CHELTENHAM
Charlton Kings
Leckhampton
Shurdington

GLOUCESTER
GLEVVM
Brockworth
Upton St Leonards
Birdlip
Cowley
Withington
Chedworth Roman Villa
NORTHL

Painswick
Bisley
Miserden
Rendcomb
North Cerney

STROUD
Stonehouse
King's Stanley
Woodchester
Minchinhampton
Chalford
Sapperton
Daglingworth

CIRENCESTER
CORINIVM
ROMAN AMPHITHEATRE
Preston
Siddington

NAILSWORTH
Avening
Tetbury
Kemble
South Cerney
Ashton Keynes
Thames Path

TETBURY
Westonbirt Arboretum
A433
Crudwell
Minety
Purton

MALMESBURY
Sherston
Brinkworth
CRICKLADE

Numbered markers: 16, 21, 20, 13, 19, 9, 8, 5, 3, 25, 4, 11, 27, 1

Keymap 2

21 · **12** · **6** · **23** · **24** · **25** · **17** · **4** · **11**

Belas Knap Long Barrow · Abbots · Guiting Power · Naunton · Maugersbury · Oddington · Kingham · Sarsden · B4450

ENHAM · Beckhampton · Hawling · Upper Slaughter · A429 · Icomb · Bledington · Foscot · Nether Abbey · Lyneham · A361

Whittington · Syreford · Hampen · Salperton · Lower Slaughter · Bourton-on-the-Water · Wyck Rissington · Westcote · Church Westcote · Bruern · Milton under Wychwood · Shipton under Wychwoo

Upper Dowdeswell · Andoversford · Shipton · Hazleton · Turkdean · Cold Aston · Notgrove · Little Rissington · Upper Rissington · Idbury · Fifield

Foxcote · Withington · Compton Abdale · Hampnett · Clapton-on-the-Hill · Farmington · Great Rissington · Sherborne · A424

Chedworth Roman Villa · Yanworth · NORTHLEACH · Eastington · Lodge Park · Great Barrington · Little Barrington · BURFORD · Asthall · Minst Love

Chedworth · Fossebridge · Coln St Dennis · Calcot · Aldsworth · Westwell · Holwell · Shilton · Swinbrook · Fordwells

Rendcomb · Woodmancote · North Cerney · Calmsden · Coln Rogers · Winson · Ablington · River Leach · Bradwell Grove · CARTERTON · Black Bourton

Bagendon · A429 · Arlington · Barnsley · Bibury · Coln St Aldwyns · Eastleach Turville · Eastleach Martin · Filkins · Kencot · Broadwell · Clanfield

AKEMAN STREET · Quenington · Hatherop · Fyfield · Southrop · Broughton Poggs · Langford · Friar's Court · Radcot

CIRENCESTER · A417 · Ampney Crucis · Ampney St Mary · Poulton · FAIRFORD · Little Faringdon · Grafton · Kelmscott · Eaton Hastings

Preston · Harnhill · Ampney St Peter · Driffield · Horcott · LECHLADE ON THAMES · Kelmscott Manor · Buscot · A4095

Siddington · Meysey Hampton · Whelford · Cotswold Water Park (Fairford/Lechlade Section) · Inglesham · Buscot Park · FARINGDON

Ewen · South Cerney · Marston Meysey · Dunfield · Kempsford · Upper Inglesham · Badbury Hill · A420

Shorncote · Somerford Keynes · Down Ampney · Latton · Castle Eaton · Hannington Wick · Coleshill · Great Coxwell · Little Coxwell

Thames Path · Ashton Keynes · Cerney Wick · Hannington · Broad Blunsdon · HIGHWORTH · B4019 · Fernham · Longcot

Upper Minety · Minety · CRICKLADE · A419 · Stanton Fitzwarren · South Marston · Sevenhampton · Watchfield · Shrivenham

Purton · Purton Stoke · Blunsdon St Andrew · Haydon Wick · Stratton St Margaret · Bourton · Woolstone · Compton Beauchamp · Uffington Castle

WOOTTON BASSETT · M4 · A3102 · Green Hill · Lydiard Millicent · Lydiard Park · Hook · SWINDON · Wanborough · Hinton Parva · Ashbury · Idstone · Bishopstone

Brinkworth · Callow Hill · Grittenham · Liddington · Badbury · Ashdown House · Wayland's Smithy · Lambourn Downs

Lyneham · Tockenham Wick · Tockenham · Church End · Elcombe · Overton · WROUGHTON · Liddington Castle · Upper Upham · Baydon · Aldbourne

Preston · Bushton · Chiseldon · Woodsend · Membury Services · Lambourn Woodlands

Goatacre · Clyffe Pypard · Broad Town · White Horse · Uffcott · Ridgeway · Ramsbury · Whittonditch

Hilmarton · Clevancy · Broad Hinton · Barbury Castle · Ogbourne St George · Chilton Foliat

Highway · Winterbourne Bassett · Berwick Bassett · Winterbourne Monkton · Marlborough Downs · White Horse · Ogbourne St Andrew · A346

A3102 · Compton Bassett · Yatesbury · Windmill Hill · Rockley · Ogbourne Maizey · Axford

CALNE · Cherhill · Avebury · Avebury Stone Circles, West Kennett Stone Avenue · A346

Quemerford · White Horse Oldbury · Avebury Trusloe · Beck

Calstone Wellington · Silbury Hill · Castle ROAD · Kennett · Forest · Chapel

Blackland · Morgan's Hill · Long Barrow · Roman Road · A346 · Great Bedwyn · Bagshot

Heddington · Roundway Hill · Wansdyke · Tan Hill · Milk Hill · Ridge Way · Cadley · Clench Common · Durley · Crofton · Little Bedwyn

Roundway · White Horse · Bishops Cannings · Allington · Alton Barnes White Horse · Alton Barnes · Huish · West Stowell · Wootton Rivers · Oare · Stibb · Crofton Beam Engines · Shalbour

SCALE 1:277 777 or 1 INCH to about 4½ MILES *1CM to 2.7KM*

KILOMETRES: 0 · 5 · 10 · 15
MILES: 0 · 2 · 4 · 6 · 8 · 10

KEYMAP HEIGHTS SHOWN IN METRES

Walk	Page	Start	Nat. Grid Reference	Distance	Time	Highest Point
Adlestrop, Evenlode and Chastleton	44	Adlestrop	SP 241271	6 miles (9.7km)	3 hrs	571ft (174m)
Avon Valley	66	Saltford	ST 686673	7 miles (11.3km)	3½ hrs	755ft (230m)
Banbury, Oxford Canal and Broughton	79	Banbury Cross	SP 453403	10 miles (16km)	4½ hrs	469ft (143m)
Brockhampton, Sevenhampton and Whittington	63	Whittington village	SP 014209	5¾ miles (9.2km)	3 hrs	853ft (260m)
Charlbury	26	Charlbury	SP 357194	6 miles (9.7km)	3 hrs	509ft (155m)
Chipping Campden and Broad Campden	16	Chipping Campden	SP 151391	4½ miles (7.2km)	2 hrs	525ft (160m)
Cirencester and the Duntisbourne Valley	75	Cirencester	SP 023020	8½ miles (13.7km)	4½ hrs	522ft (159m)
Coates and the source of the Thames	18	Coates village centre	SO 978008	3 miles (4.8km)	1½ hrs	459ft (140m)
Crickley Hill and Leckhampton Hill	60	Crickley Hill Country Park	SO 930163	7 miles (11.3km)	3½ hrs	951ft (290m)
Deerhurst, Apperley and the River Severn	49	Deerhurst	SO 869298	7 miles (11.3km)	3½ hrs	164ft (50m)
Dursley, Uley and Owlpen	87	Dursley	ST 756981	8½ miles (13.7km)	4½ hrs	722ft (220m)
Edgeworth and Pinbury Park	28	Edgeworth	SO 945063	5½ miles (8.9km)	3 hrs	689ft (210m)
Lechlade, Kelmscott and the River Thames	52	Lechlade	SU 214995	7½ miles (12.1km)	3½ hrs	236ft (72m)
Longborough, Sezincote and Bourton-on-the-Hill	32	Longborough	SP 178296	5½ miles (8.9km)	2½ hrs	591ft (180m)
Macaroni Downs and the Leach Valley	72	Eastleach Turville	SP 198052	7½ miles (12.1km)	4 hrs	476ft (145m)
Malmesbury and the River Avon	14	Malmesbury, Old Station Yard	ST 932874	2 miles (3.2km)	1 hr	246ft (75m)
Milton under Wychwood and Fifield	38	Milton under Wychwood	SP 264183	6 miles (9.7km)	3 hrs	492ft (150m)
Miserden and Winstone	30	Miserden	SO 937088	5 miles (8km)	2½ hrs	804ft (245m)
Northleach and Farmington	24	Northleach	SP 113146	5 miles (8km)	2½ hrs	636ft (194m)
Nympsfield and Hetty Pegler's Tump	22	Nympsfield village	SO 800005	3 miles (4.8km)	1½ hrs	764ft (233m)
Painswick and the Beacon	58	Painswick	SO 865096	6 miles (9.7km)	3 hrs	928ft (283m)
Seven Springs and the Churn Valley	41	Seven Springs	SO 967170	6 miles (9.7km)	3 hrs	886ft (270m)
Sharpness and Berkeley	46	Sharpness	SO 667021	6½ miles (10.5km)	3 hrs	82ft (25m)
Sherborne and the River Windrush	69	Sherborne Park	SP 159143	7½ miles (12.1km)	3½ hrs	591ft (180m)
Somerford Keynes and the River Thames	35	Cotswold Water Park	SU 028959	6 miles (9.7km)	3 hrs	305ft (93m)
Stow-on-the-Wold, Broadwell and Donnington	55	Stow-on-the-Wold	SP 191258	6 miles (9.7km)	3 hrs	705ft (215m)
Tetbury and Westonbirt	83	Tetbury	ST 891931	9½ miles (15.3km)	4½ hrs	469ft (143m)
Thames and Severn Canal and Cerney Wick	20	Cotswold Visitor Information Centre	SU 071970	4½ miles (7.2km)	2½ hrs	295ft (90m)

Comments

Both Adlestrop and Evenlode are delightful villages that overlook the Evenlode Valley, and the route passes by a splendid 17th-century manor house.

There are distant views of both Bath and Bristol from the higher points on this route, which also includes a stretch along a disused railway track and some pleasant riverside walking.

After an opening stretch along the towpath of the Oxford Canal, the route heads across fields to Broughton Castle before returning to Banbury.

A walk amid the rolling wold country of the upper Coln Valley that takes in three villages and some fine views.

A fairly flat walk of wide and extensive views across the valley of the River Evenlode, including the wooded slopes of Wychwood Forest towards the end.

For much of this route the tower of Chipping Campden's famous 'wool church' is in sight.

The Duntisbourne Valley is followed from Cirencester, through Stratton, Daglingworth and on to the secluded and idyllic hamlet of Duntisbourne Rouse.

The long abandoned Thames and Severn Canal forms the backdrop to this delightfully varied walk which offers an optional spur to the source of the Thames.

Both Crickley Hill and Leckhampton Hill occupy the Cotswold escarpment and provide outstanding views over Cheltenham and the Vale of Severn.

The two Saxon churches at Deerhurst are of great historic interest, and the walk ends with a lovely ramble beside the River Severn.

After an energetic opening stretch along the Cotswold escarpment between Dursley and Uley, the remainder of the walk is fairly flat, returning to the town through woodland.

You pass a medieval church, two manor houses and make two descents into the thickly wooded valley of the River Frome.

Most of this flat walk in the upper Thames Valley between Lechlade and Kelmscott is across meadows, either close to or beside the river.

The walk links two attractive villages and passes close to an unusual country house, built to resemble an Indian palace.

Two beautiful, adjacent villages are at the start of this walk, which takes you through the valley of the little River Leach and onto the Macaroni Downs.

This short and easy walk mainly follows the meandering River Avon across meadows below the abbey town of Malmesbury.

There are some superb areas of woodland and wide views across the Evenlode Valley. The walk also passes close to a large country house.

Between Miserden and Winstone, the route descends into the well-wooded Frome Valley and passes through part of Misarden Park.

You can combine a fine scenic walk with a visit to the church at Northleach, one of the grandest of Cotswold 'wool churches'.

The walk starts in a pretty Cotswold village, visits a prehistoric barrow and includes several stretches through peaceful woodland.

There are plenty of 'ups and downs' on this walk but none of them is particularly steep or strenuous. The views from Painswick Beacon are outstanding.

From Seven Springs, the noise of the heavy traffic is soon left behind, and you pass through two quiet villages on this undemanding walk in the Churn Valley.

After heading inland from the Severn Estuary to Berkeley, you return to the river for a final stretch alongside the estuary. There are fine views of the Forest of Dean.

After descending through the woodlands of Sherborne Park into the village, the route continues first by Sherborne Brook and later by the River Windrush before returning to the start.

There are wide views across some of the lakes of the Cotswold Water Park, and part of the route is alongside the infant River Thames.

This walk in typical wold country starts and finishes in one of the most appealing of Cotswold towns.

A lengthy but generally flat walk which takes you from Tetbury to the superb woodlands of Westonbirt Arboretum.

A flat walk in the Cotswold Water Park that uses both a disused railway track and the towpath of a disused canal.

At-a-glance...

Introduction to More Cotswold Walks

This second *Pathfinder* title on the Cotswolds covers the same area as the first
title, except that this area is extended slightly westwards to include two walks
in the Vale of Severn. This is to add greater variety to the selection of routes.

Nowhere else in the country do the work of nature and the work of man
appear to be in greater harmony than in the Cotswolds. There are other parts of
England that possess more dramatic scenery and there are equally attractive
villages in other regions, but here is a combination of idyllic stone villages and
small towns set amid a gentle, rolling countryside that is without parallel and
quintessentially 'English'.

How has this uniquely attractive combination been created and largely
preserved? To explain this we need to examine three major factors relating to
the geology, history and geography of the region: the local stone, the development of the woollen industry and the lack of nearby coal deposits.

Local stone

The Cotswolds form part of a line of uplands, composed of oolitic limestone,
that stretches in a roughly north-east to south-west direction from Yorkshire to
Dorset. *Wold* is a Saxon word meaning 'upland'; the origin of *cot* is more
difficult to establish. One theory is that it comes from the Saxon word for sheep
enclosure; an alternative suggestion is that it is derived from *Cod*, the name of
a Saxon chief who settled in the upper Windrush valley. Possibly the name
Cotswold originally may have referred only to the area around the Windrush,
later extended to cover the whole of this upland region.

Unlike the carboniferous limestone of the Yorkshire Dales and the Mendips,
oolitic limestone does not create deep gorges and underground cave systems
but a more intimate and less dramatic landscape characterised by rolling hills
and gentle valleys. The Cotswolds tilt slightly to the south-east, thereby
thrusting up a bold and often steep escarpment on their western edge. From
this escarpment a succession of fine viewpoints – Dover's Hill, Broadway
Tower, Cleeve Common, Cooper's Hill, Haresfield Beacon, Wotton Hill and
Hinton Hill – look westwards over the lowlands of the vales of Evesham,
Gloucester and Berkeley to the equally bold outlines of the Malverns, Shrop-
shire Hills and Black Mountains on the distant horizon. Nearer at hand the eye
is drawn to a number of individual outlying hills detached from the main
Cotswold range; two of the most prominent of these are Bredon Hill near
Evesham and Robins Wood Hill overlooking Gloucester.

Behind the escarpment lies the long 'dip' slope. Here is the typical rolling
wold country which drops gently to the formerly extensive royal hunting
ground of Wychwood Forest and merges almost imperceptibly into the flat

country of the Oxford Plain. In the north of the region a number of rivers with delightful-sounding names – Evenlode, Windrush, Leach, Coln – have cut wide valleys through the wolds, flowing south-eastwards into the plain eventually to join the Thames, a Cotswold river in its origin. Only in the south, in the narrower valleys around Stroud, do the rivers flow westwards to the Severn. Uniquely among Cotswold rivers, the Bristol Avon describes a great arc, flowing first eastwards, then turning southwards and finally curving westwards through Bradford-on-Avon and on to Bath, to form an obvious southern boundary to the Cotswolds. The northern edge is less clearly defined but here the line of limestone uplands descends to the valley of another River Avon, the Warwickshire or Shakespeare's Avon.

Cotswold stone makes excellent building material and has been used extensively for this purpose. One of its most appealing features is the variation in colour shades, which can range, depending on area, from light grey through pale cream, yellow, honey and deep golden to light brown. It is above all the quality and colour of this limestone, which invariably looks warm on even the dullest day, which makes the villages and small towns of the region so attractive. So well do some of the smaller villages blend into their natural surroundings that they seem to be an integral part of the landscape.

Woollen industry

In his *Britannia,* published in 1610, William Camden says of the Cotswolds: 'In these Woulds there feed, in great numbers, flockes of sheepe'. If the local limestone produced the basic material for the buildings of the region, it was the prosperity generated initially by these 'flockes of sheepe' that provided the money for them. Much of the rich architectural heritage of the Cotswolds comes from the development of the medieval wool trade.

Sheep-farming began with the first human inhabitants of the region. With their dry slopes and sheltered valleys, the Cotswolds were a popular area for settlement from earliest times and a large number of varied prehistoric monuments survive. Among the best-known and most impressive of these are the burial chamber at Belas Knap, the group of remains known collectively as the Rollright Stones, and the Iron Age fortifications, which made use of the high vantage points. The summits of Bredon Hill, Cleeve Hill and Haresfield Beacon are among many that are crowned with such defensive earthworks but the most elaborate and extensive are those that occupy the plateau of Minchinhampton Common above the Frome and Nailsworth valleys.

The Romans found the area congenial and relatively easy to penetrate. They established Corinium (Cirencester) as one of their principal cities and Aquae Sulis (Bath) as their major health resort, building a number of villas, for example at Chedworth and Witcombe, and constructing a series of roads – Foss Way, Ermin Street, Akeman Street – across the region. After the Romans came the Anglo-Saxons, who founded most of the present-day settlements and later introduced Christianity. Last in the line of conquerors were the Normans, who

Cotswold Water Park, near Cerney Wick

in the years after 1066 rebuilt many of the churches, established strong castles on the fringes of the region at Oxford and Gloucester and also created the royal forest of Wychwood, which lies around Burford, Charlbury and Woodstock. It was the monastic foundations of the Cotswolds (Cirencester, Winchcombe, Hailes) that helped to pioneer the development of the wool trade, which reached its peak between the 14th and 17th centuries. At first the raw wool was exported to the continent but in the early 14th century Edward III imported weavers from Flanders to develop a native cloth industry. Over the next few centuries the manufacturing of woollen cloth expanded and prospered and by the end of the Middle Ages it had become England's major export industry. Half of it was produced in the Cotswolds, where the advantages of an abundance of sheep, water power and good communications ensured the predominance of the region.

It is from this heyday of the cloth trade that the distinguished architectural legacy of the area – domestic, commercial and religious – chiefly dates. This includes comparatively humble buildings, like small village churches, farmhouses, market halls and the modest but dignified houses and cottages that adorn such delightful places as Castle Combe, Bourton-on-the-Water and Bibury, as well as the grander town houses of wool merchants and the manor houses at Minster Lovell, Snowshill and Chastleton. Particularly outstanding are the magnificent 15th-century 'wool churches', endowed by wealthy wool magnates like William Grevel of Chipping Campden and the Forteys of Northleach. All visitors will have their favourites, but probably the most impressive are those that rise above Cirencester, Winchcombe, Burford, Chipping Campden and Northleach.

Lack of coal

It is fortunate that much of this rich legacy has survived relatively intact and unspoilt and this is largely due to the absence of local coal deposits. With the onset of the Industrial Revolution, and in particular the application of first water- and later steam-powered machinery, the Cotswold woollen industry declined, unable to compete with the textile areas on the slopes of the Pennines, which had the advantages of faster-flowing streams and proximity to coal. Only the area around Stroud, where the streams are fast flowing, was able to expand and prolong its status as an important cloth-producing region into the early 19th century, until it also lost out to the more powerful woollen industries of Yorkshire. Here the narrow valleys, with their steep sides covered in tiers of houses and with 19th-century mills in the valley bottoms, rather resemble the Pennine valleys of Lancashire and Yorkshire – except that they never became extensively urbanised and industrialised.

Throughout the region the decline of the woollen industry led to much hardship and poverty – it is difficult to conceive of such an obviously prosperous area as this ever suffering hardship – but paradoxically it was this that was largely instrumental in preserving the attractiveness of the Cotswolds. Relative economic stagnation prevented the large-scale rebuilding, urbanisation and inevitable environmental damage that scarred so many other parts of Britain during the era of the Industrial Revolution.

In time a regeneration took place, largely based on the permanent advantages of the region – its climate, countryside and accessibility – that made it an attractive place to live and later a popular tourist area. A number of great country houses were built during the 18th and 19th centuries, including Cornbury Park, Blenheim Palace and Sezincote. In the late Georgian and Regency periods Cheltenham prospered and expanded as a fashionable spa and residential town. William Morris, the influential Victorian arbiter of taste and social reformer, helped to start off the tourist industry by popularising such beauty spots as Bibury and Broadway. During the 20th century the car has opened up the whole area to many more visitors and now tourism has become a vital part of the economy of the Cotswolds.

In Shakespeare's *Richard II* the Cotswolds are described as 'high wild hills and rough uneven ways', but in the main this is no longer true. Apart from a few remaining unenclosed 'wild' areas such as Cleeve Common, this is an intimate and largely tamed landscape where the man-made features of churches, villages, farms and manor houses fit snugly into their physical surroundings of hills and valleys, fields and woodlands. By far the best way to explore and appreciate at first hand this uniquely beautiful and harmonious corner of England is on foot and an extensive network of waymarked paths enables you to do that – an immensely rewarding and pleasurable experience.

With the introduction of **'gps enabled' walks,** you will see that this book now includes a list of waypoints alongside the description of the walk. We have included these so that you can enjoy the full benefits of gps should you wish to. Gps is an amazingly useful and entertaining navigational aid, and you do not need to be computer literate to enjoy it.

GPS waypoint co-ordinates add value to your walk. You will now have the extra advantage of introducing 'direction' into your walking which will enhance your leisure walking and make it safer. Use of a gps brings greater confidence and security and you will find you cover ground a lot faster should you need to.

For more detailed information on using your gps, a *Pathfinder Guide* introducing you to gps and digital mapping is now available. *GPS for Walkers*, written by experienced gps teacher and navigation trainer Clive Thomas, is available in bookshops (ISBN 978-0-7117-4445-5) or order online at www.totalwalking.co.uk

Malmesbury and the River Avon

		GPS waypoints
Start	Malmesbury, Old Station Yard car park	🖉 ST 932 874
Distance	2 miles (3.2km)	Ⓐ ST 936 875
Approximate time	1 hour	Ⓑ ST 935 868
Parking	Old Station Yard car park at Malmesbury	Ⓒ ST 930 872
Refreshments	Pubs and cafés at Malmesbury	
Ordnance Survey maps	Landranger 173 (Swindon & Devizes), Explorer 168 (Stroud, Tetbury & Malmesbury)	

Malmesbury occupies a hilltop site above the water meadows of the River Avon, and this short walk is across some of these meadows, following the various branches of the river around the edge of the town. It uses part of the Malmesbury Riverwalk, established by the local civic trust in the 1970s, which consists of a mixture of public and permissive footpaths. The succession of attractive views of the town are inevitably dominated by the still impressive ruins of its once great abbey.

🖉 With your back to the river, turn right across the picnic area and a few paces from a road junction, pass through a kissing-gate to walk along a tree-lined path beside the river. Go through a kissing-gate and keep ahead to a road by the Spice Merchant restaurant Ⓐ.

Turn right to cross the bridge over the river, immediately turn left down steps, climb a stile and follow a path across meadows, bearing right to the corner. Climb two stiles in quick succession, bear left and head diagonally across the next meadow. Cross a footbridge, keep ahead to a road and turn right. The road (Baskerville) curves left to a T-junction by the old almshouses of St John's Hospital.

Turn left, cross the Avon by the imposing Avon Mills, former silk mills built in the 1790s, and just after following the road round a right-hand bend, turn right through a gate Ⓑ onto a permissive path. Climb a stile, keep along the right-hand edge of a meadow and, after going through a kissing-gate, keep ahead to emerge briefly onto the right-hand edge of a sloping field. Continue into trees, cross two footbridges, go through a kissing-gate and walk across a meadow to another kissing-gate. Keep ahead alongside a hedge on the right, pass through a gap into the next meadow and turn right onto a paved path Ⓒ, first crossing a bridge over a minor channel and then turning right to cross the main river.

Walk along a walled tarmac path to a road and turn right (Burnivale) heading uphill. Turn left to ascend steps, bear right and continue up into the town centre of Malmesbury, a pleasant little town with a number of attractive streets and buildings. Although only about one-third of its original size, the Benedictine abbey, founded in the 7th century, is still a most imposing building. The present church, mainly comprising part of the nave, was built in the 12th century and is entered by a magnificent Norman porch. Inside is the tomb of the Saxon king Athelstan. Look out in the churchyard for an epitaph on a tomb-

stone that records the unusual death of a woman in 1703, mauled by a tiger which had escaped from a travelling circus that had been visiting the town.

Turn left, passing to the left of the abbey, and just past the Old Bell Hotel turn right into Mill Lane. Head down-hill, curving left to cross a bridge over the river, and turn left to return to the start. ●

Malmesbury

Chipping Campden and Broad Campden

		GPS waypoints
Start	Chipping Campden	🖊 SP 151 391
Distance	4½ miles (7.2km)	Ⓐ SP 157 394
Approximate time	2 hours	Ⓑ SP 154 390
Parking	Roadside parking at Chipping Campden	Ⓒ SP 160 377
		Ⓓ SP 158 378
Refreshments	Pubs and cafés at Chipping Campden, pub at Broad Campden	
Ordnance Survey maps	Landranger 151 (Stratford-upon-Avon), Explorer OL45 (The Cotswolds)	

Most of this short and easy walk is across the meadows and fields that lie to the south of Chipping Campden, between this small town and the neighbouring village of Broad Campden. The highlights of the route are the many fine views across the fields of the tower of Chipping Campden's superb 'wool church'.

With its wealth of mellowed, grey and cream stone houses, 17th-century Market Hall and 15th-century church, Chipping Campden is the Cotswold wool town *par excellence*. Its dignified curving High Street is acclaimed as one of the finest in the country, a superb essay in harmony with diversity, with buildings of all ages from the 14th century onwards – but mostly a reflection of the town's prosperity in the 'golden age' of the Cotswold wool trade, in the later Middle Ages and on into the 16th and 17th centuries. The church is a magnificent example of a 'wool church', its Perpendicular tower dominating the town. Inside are monuments to some of Chipping Campden's wool merchants, including William Grevel, whose 14th-century house still stands in the High Street, and Sir Baptist Hicks, a 17th-century cloth merchant and first Viscount Campden (d. 1629), who was responsible for two of the town's most

admired pieces of architecture: the delightful row of almshouses (1612) just below the church and the Market Hall (1627).

🖊 Start by the Market Hall and walk along the main street towards the church. Take the first road on the right, which curves left to the church, and turn right along Station Road. At a public footpath sign – and a National Trust sign 'The Coneygree' – turn right Ⓐ over a stone stile and walk straight across the Coneygree, an area of meadowland bought by the National Trust to preserve the surroundings of the church.

Head downhill, at the bottom cross a footbridge, turn right and walk diagonally across a field. After crossing another footbridge, turn sharp left Ⓑ and head across the next field to go through a galvanised gate in the corner. Continue to the next galvanised gate and now the path divides. There is a stile opposite and a gate to the right of it. Aim for the latter and head diagonally up the slope and down the far side to the fence corner. Keep going diagonally right as the field broadens out and make for a galvanised kissing-gate over in the hedge corner. Walk along the right-hand edge of the field for a short distance, pass into the field on the right and then swing left to keep a brook on the left. Cross a stile in the field corner, then the brook, and head uphill on the field path. Keep the hedgerow on the right and walk along to a stile. Turn right and follow the track beyond some stone buildings. Cross a stile by a cattle-grid, approach Broad Campden and Briar Hill Farm and follow the track round to the left to the road. Turn right, and right again at the sign – unsuitable for motors – **C**. Walk up to a junction by a chapel on the right **D**, veer right

and at the immediate fork, keep left, passing in front of a row of cottages.

Where the track ends by an 18th-century Quaker meeting house, bear left along an enclosed path to a kissing-gate. Go through and continue along a path, crossing a drive in front of a large cottage. Go through another kissing-gate and keep ahead across a large field, following the Heart of England Way. Ahead the houses and church tower of Chipping Campden come into view.

The path bears left to continue across the field, then keeps along its left-hand edge – parallel to a road – to reach a track. Turn left towards the road but immediately turn right along a tarmac track (George Lane) and follow it into Chipping Campden. Where the track ends, keep ahead in a straight line – first along a road, then between houses, and finally through a car park and under an arch – to emerge onto the main street just to the left of the Market Hall. ●

SCALE 1:25000 or 2½ INCHES to 1 MILE 4CM to 1KM

```
0    200   400   600   800 METRES   1
                                    KILOMETRES
                                    MILES
0    200   400   600 YARDS   ½
```

Coates and the source of the Thames

		GPS waypoints
Start	Coates	
Distance	3 miles (4.8km)	✏ SO 978 008
Approximate time	1½ hours	Ⓐ SO 972 010
Parking	Roadside parking in Coates	Ⓑ SO 979 000
Refreshments	The Tunnel House pub by the Thames and Severn Canal	
Ordnance Survey maps	Landranger 163 (Cheltenham & Cirencester) Explorer 168 (Stroud, Tetbury & Malmesbury)	

Two of the region's most historic waterways form the theme to this delightful walk to the west of Cirencester. Beginning with a very pleasant stretch of farmland walking, the route heads for the abandoned Thames and Severn Canal, much of it hidden by a thick curtain of trees and foliage. A short, optional spur at the eastern end of the waterway brings you to the source of the Thames, England's greatest river. The stone marking the spot is a vivid reminder of the contrast between the river's source in a peaceful Gloucestershire meadow and its spectacular journey through the heart of London.

✏ With your back to the village hall turn left and walk along to May Tree Close where there is a post box and a telephone box.

Turn left and follow the footpath along to a gate. Cross the field towards trees, making for a gate at the point where a path crosses the route of the walk. Continue ahead in the next field with trees and bushes on your left. Head for a gate in the field corner and continue along the edge of the next pasture to a gate leading out to a road. Cross over and take the concrete farm track ahead. Pass St Matthew's church Ⓐ – its tower and chancel were built between 1316 and 1361 and the south doorway has a Norman arch – and continue to the farm outbuildings next

door. When the track swings right, go straight on beside a stone wall. Keep ahead into the next field and continue on the clear grassy path. Make for a gap in a stone wall and continue in the same direction across the next field. Head for a kissing-gate on the far side and walk down some steps to a railway line. Cross it to a kissing-gate and keep to the right-hand side of a paddock to a gate. Go forward, following a track towards the Tunnel House pub. As you approach it, swing left and descend steps to reach the towpath of the Thames and Severn Canal. On the left is the entrance to the Sapperton Tunnel, which when built in the 1780s was the longest tunnel ever dug in the country. This stretch of the canal was abandoned in 1927.

The Tunnel House pub near Coates

Keep the canal on your left and pass one of several round houses on the canal. Pass under the railway and continue on the towpath, following it between trees and lines of vegetation. At the next bridge **B** leave the towpath by turning right to follow a track. Cross a ladder-stile and continue across fields with woodland on the left. Cross the next ladder-stile and spot a barn on the hillside ahead. Keep going to the next gate and stile and walk ahead for about 125 yds keeping over towards the left boundary. Look for an ash tree beneath which is a stone marking the source of the River Thames.

From here return to the Thames and Severn Canal, cross the waterway and keep some stone barns on the right. Follow the track up the slope and across the fields. As it bends left cross a stone stile into the next field and keep ahead with a wall on your left. Make for a stone stile leading out to the road, turn left and walk along to a sign for the recycling site. Turn right here and return to the start. ●

Thames and Severn Canal and Cerney Wick

Start	Cotswold Visitor Information Centre, Cotswold Water Park
Distance	4½ miles (7.2km)
Approximate time	2½ hours
Parking	Car park by Cotswold Visitor Information Centre
Refreshments	Café at Information Centre, pub at Cerney Wick
Ordnance Survey maps	Landranger 163 (Cheltenham & Cirencester), Explorer 169 (Cirencester & Swindon)

GPS waypoints

- 🖉 SU 071 970
- Ⓐ SU 078 960
- Ⓑ SU 070 955
- Ⓒ SU 063 963
- Ⓓ SU 057 971
- Ⓔ SU 054 974

The track of a disused railway and the towpath of a disused canal are utilised to create an attractive and absorbing walk in the Cotswold Water Park. There is some superb woodland, fine views across lakes and the historic interest provided by abandoned railway bridges and canal locks. It is possible that in winter the last leg of the walk might be flooded. To avoid it use alternative paths.

🖉 Begin by keeping your back to the Information Centre. Turn right and head south. Continue by the left-hand edge of a lake and at the far end bear left in the corner of a meadow to enter woodland. Cross a footbridge and turn right to continue beside the dried-up bed of the canal. After passing the 18th century Round House on the other side of the canal – built for employees of the canal company – the path reaches a lane Ⓐ. Turn right into Cerney Wick, at a junction by the Crown Inn keep ahead over a stile, walk along the left field edge and climb a stile in the corner onto a narrow lane. Go through a gate opposite, walk along the right-hand edge of a field, go through another gate, climb another stile and keep ahead along a wooden walkway, continuing along the edge of a meadow beside a

lake. As the track curves right, veer left down steps into trees. Cross a footbridge, walk along the left-hand edge of a meadow, climb a stile in the corner and turn right, at a public footpath sign to South Cerney and Ashford Keynes, to join a disused railway track Ⓑ. This used to be part of the Midland Junction Railway, which ran between Cheltenham and Southampton. Turn right and follow it for just over ½ mile to a road. Cross over to a car park and the fine brick arches of the abandoned railway are an indication that the next stage of the walk is also along the old track bed which was converted into a footpath and cycleway after the railway closed in the 1960s.

Go through a gate in the corner of the car park Ⓒ, following the path signposted South Cerney and Lakes. Walk along an enclosed, hedge-lined track, passing between lakes on both sides, and ultimately it follows the road by South Cerney Sailing Club. Where the road curves left into South Cerney, turn sharp right through a gate and walk along an enclosed path. The path bends left to pass under a disused bridge, bends right beside the brick arches and turns left at a fence corner **D** to continue in a straight line, between garden fences on the left and woodland on the right. After briefly emerging by the side of a road, the path continues along the right-hand edge of a playing field, crosses the River Churn and keeps ahead along a lovely tree-lined avenue to pass under the brick arches of another disused railway bridge.

Immediately turn left beside the bridge, cross a plank footbridge and climb steps, bending left up to a lane. Turn left to cross the bridge **E**, walk along the narrow lane as far as a public footpath sign to Cerney Wick and turn right along a hedge-lined track. On the left is the bed of the disused Thames and Severn Canal, built between 1783 and 1789 to link the two great river systems. It was never commercially successful and was finally abandoned in the 1920s, although stretches are currently being restored. Where the track turns right to a farm, keep ahead to climb a stile and continue along another lovely tree-lined path – still by the disused canal – to eventually reach a galvanised gate by a former lock in front of a bridge. Pass through it and then the next gate before heading for the road bridge. Cross the road to the car park where the walk began. ●

Nympsfield and Hetty Pegler's Tump

		GPS waypoints
Start	Nympsfield	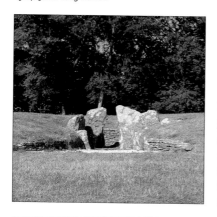 SO 800 005
Distance	3 miles (4.8km)	Ⓐ SO 800 003
Approximate time	1½ hours	Ⓑ ST 792 995
Parking	Nympsfield village centre	Ⓒ SO 792 000
Refreshments	Pub at Nympsfield	
Ordnance Survey maps	Landranger 162 (Gloucester & Forest of Dean), Explorer 168 (Stroud, Tetbury & Malmesbury)	

There is a strong prehistoric theme to this walk as it passes one of the region's best-known neolithic long barrows, situated on the Cotswold escarpment. The route begins in the village of Nympsfield before heading for attractive wooded countryside to the south west. After visiting the long barrow, return to Nympsfield by a parallel permissive path.

From the centre of Nympsfield keep right at the fork by the Rose and Crown and follow the lane through the village.

About 100 yds before reaching the church – mostly 18th century apart from the Perpendicular tower – turn right over a stone stile Ⓐ. Head gently uphill and climb a stone stile in the top

Nympsfield Long Barrow

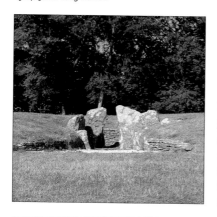

right-hand corner of the field onto a road.

Climb the stile opposite, head downhill across grass and follow a path into trees to a stile. Climb it, continue quite steeply downhill through woodland and at the bottom where there are three paths take the middle waymarked route, following it to a stile. Continue along the edge of farmland, with trees on the right, to the next stile and then keep ahead on the enclosed path along the woodland edge. Merge with another path and keep alongside woodland.

On reaching a junction of paths by a stile on the left, turn sharp right Ⓑ and head steeply uphill. Bear right on joining another path and continue less steeply up, finally curving left beside a metal gate onto the road. Turn right and at a sign to Uley Long Barrow, turn left Ⓒ onto a path that keeps along the right-hand edge of a field to the barrow.

Nympsfield

Nicknamed 'Hetty Pegler's Tump', this prehistoric burial mound is around the same age as the one near the start of the walk. It is about 180ft (55m) long and comprises a stone-built central passage with two chambers either side and a third one at the end.

Return to the road, turn right and walk back to the metal gate. Twenty yards beyond it veer left onto a woodland path and when it forks take the higher path. Begin climbing and eventually you merge with another path. Follow it to a stile, head uphill to the road and turn left, then right for Nympsfield. Walk along to the village centre where the walk began. ●

Northleach and Farmington

		GPS waypoints
Start	Northleach	SP 113 146
Distance	5 miles (8km)	Ⓐ SP 116 147
Approximate time	2½ hours	Ⓑ SP 126 151
Parking	Northleach, Market Place	Ⓒ SP 137 152
Refreshments	Pubs and cafés at Northleach	Ⓓ SP 139 147
Ordnance Survey maps	Landranger 163 (Cheltenham & Cirencester), Explorer OL45 (The Cotswolds)	Ⓔ SP 134 139
		Ⓕ SP 114 138

This walk in the Leach Valley takes you along a mixture of lanes, field paths and tracks between Northleach and the hilltop village of Farmington. There are extensive views across rolling wold country, and the tower of the famous 'wool church' at Northleach is in sight for much of the final ¹⁄₂ mile.

The 15th-century church at Northleach, with its magnificent south porch, is acclaimed as one of the grandest among the many grand 'wool churches' of the Cotswolds, its imposing Perpendicular tower dominating the streets of the attractive small town. It reflects the heyday of the wool trade; inside are many monuments to the great wool merchants who created the town's prosperity. Handsome stone and half-timbered buildings line the High Street, and the inns are a reminder of Northleach's importance in the days of coach travel.

Start in the Market Place, then on the far side of the main street, take the wide tarmac path between houses, called Doctors Lane. On emerging onto a road, turn half-right, head up between houses to a T-junction and continue uphill along an enclosed path – later through woodland – to a lane Ⓐ. Turn left along the lane,

passing under the A40, for ³⁄₄ mile and, where it bends left downhill, bear right onto a track Ⓑ.

After going through a metal gate, bear left and head gently downhill across a field, keeping more or less in line with a line of telegraph poles. Head diagonally down the field to a footbridge and stile and then go half right, passing under the cables up to a stile on the skyline. Cross it and go straight across the field. Join a track, passing to the right of Farmington church to a lane Ⓒ. The village is to the

Farmington church

left, centred around a large green and containing some handsome houses. The church is mainly Norman, with a Perpendicular tower.

The route continues to the right. Take the first lane on the right, signposted to Northleach and Burford, heading downhill, and in the dip turn right through a gate **D** at a public footpath sign, and walk across a field, parallel to a tiny brook on the right. Cross a stile, turn right to cross the brook, turn left and walk across a field. Cross a track, continue across the next field and, just before reaching the far side, turn half-right up to a waymarked gate. Go through, turn left along the left-hand field edge, climb a stile and continue along the left-hand field edge. Pass through a hedge gap by a stile in the corner, walk gently uphill along the left-hand edge of the next field and go through a gate onto the A40.

Carefully cross both the main road and a side road and follow a path through a gap in the trees to a stile. Climb it, keep ahead through woodland, climb another stile and continue straight across a field. Turn right through a metal gate **E** on the far side, keep along the right-hand edge of the fence.

Pass a corrugated barn, make for the field corner and join a tree-lined track. Go through a metal gate, head downhill along a track – passing to the left of a pool and crossing a footbridge over the outlet stream – keep ahead uphill and look out for where you turn right through a gate. Walk across a field and at a wall corner, turn left and continue up towards a large house. In the field corner go through a gate onto a lane and follow it to a T-junction.

Keep ahead along an enclosed track and after ½ mile, turn right **F** at a public footpath sign, along the left-hand edge of a field, heading gently downhill. There is a superb view ahead over Northleach, dominated by its church tower. Go through a gate, continue downhill and, in the bottom corner, turn left through a gate and turn right to pass between tennis courts on the left and a children's play area on the right. At the corner of the tennis courts, bear left to cross a footbridge over the infant River Leach and keep ahead along an enclosed tarmac path to a road. Turn left back to the Market Place. ●

Charlbury

		GPS waypoints	
Start	Charlbury	📝	SP 357 194
Distance	6 miles (9.7km)	Ⓐ	SP 361 195
Approximate time	3 hours	Ⓑ	SP 381 200
Parking	Charlbury, Spendlove Centre	Ⓒ	SP 391 188
Refreshments	Pubs and café at Charlbury	Ⓓ	SP 387 175
Ordnance Survey maps	Landranger 164 (Oxford),	Ⓔ	SP 363 187
	Explorer 180 (Oxford)	Ⓕ	SP 360 188

This is an undemanding walk, mostly along well-defined paths and broad tracks, in the gently undulating countryside of the Evenlode Valley to the east and south of Charlbury. There are a series of extensive views, especially on the latter stages of the route, looking across the valley to Cornbury Park and the wooded slopes of Wychwood Forest.

The quiet, pleasant little town of Charlbury has a fine situation on the eastern slopes of the Evenlode Valley, overlooking the wooded expanses of Wychwood Forest on the western slopes.

It was once noted for its glove-making industry and has a number of old houses dating back to the 16th and 17th centuries. Dominating the town is the tower of its medieval church.

🖊 Start in the town centre at the junction of Market Street, Church Street and Sheep Street and, facing the Bull Inn, take the road to the left of it (Browns Lane). Take the first turning on the right along the right-hand edge of a green, turn left at the end of the green and turn right along a track between houses.

Cross a road Ⓐ, continue along the tarmac track passing modern housing estates to reach a metal kissing-gate. Turn right and then bear left at the next junction where a footpath runs off to the right. Follow the clear bridleway, keeping a quarry on the left. When you reach the edge of a field with a farmhouse visible ahead, bear left along its edge and shortly the path bears round to the right to a T-junction just beyond the farm Ⓑ.

Turn sharp right along the Salt Way which is wide and rutted, and follow it to a road. Cross over and take the path opposite along the right-hand edge of a field. In the corner, turn right Ⓒ in front of a gate, pass through a gap and continue along an enclosed path. Follow this path in a more or less straight line – sometimes enclosed and sometimes along either the left- or right-hand edges of fields – as far as a crossroads. All the way there are extensive views across fields and the village seen over to the left is Stonesfield.

At the crossroads, turn right along a tarmac track Ⓓ, here joining the Oxfordshire Way. Where the track bends right by a cottage, turn first left and then almost immediately right through a blue-waymarked gate. Keep along the left-hand field edge, go through a gate and continue along an undulating track. At a blue-waymarked post, the track narrows to a path, and you continue along this attractive, tree-lined path, eventually emerging onto a track Ⓔ.

Turn left down to a road and keep ahead, following the road around a right-hand bend. At the bend, bear left along Hixet Wood Ⓕ, head first downhill and then continue up into Charlbury town centre. ●

Edgeworth and Pinbury Park

		GPS waypoints
Start	Edgeworth, at top of lane leading to Edgeworth church	SO 945 063
Distance	5½ miles (8.9km)	Ⓐ SO 947 059
Approximate time	3 hours	Ⓑ SO 961 062
Parking	Roadside parking at top of lane signposted to Edgeworth church	Ⓒ SO 968 061
		Ⓓ SO 963 053
Refreshments	None	Ⓔ SO 946 049
Ordnance Survey maps	Landranger 163 (Cheltenham & Cirencester), Explorer 168 (Stroud, Tetbury & Malmesbury)	

This pleasant route does a circuit around the deep and well-wooded Frome Valley, descending and ascending to cross the small river twice. There is a particularly attractive stretch through Pinbury Park, passing in front of the house from where there are fine views across the valley, and some outstanding views near the end of the walk of Edgeworth Manor and church.

Start by walking down the winding, undulating lane to the medieval church, which retains a fine Norman chancel and south doorway Ⓐ. Keep ahead along the drive towards

View of the Frome Valley near Edgeworth

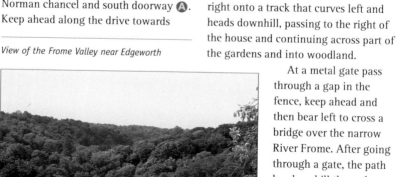

Edgeworth Manor – built in the 17th century and enlarged in the 19th century – and in front of the gates, turn right onto a track that curves left and heads downhill, passing to the right of the house and continuing across part of the gardens and into woodland.

At a metal gate pass through a gap in the fence, keep ahead and then bear left to cross a bridge over the narrow River Frome. After going through a gate, the path heads uphill through trees to a lane. Turn right as far as a crossroads, turn right, in the Sapperton and Stroud direction, and at a public bridleway sign, turn left Ⓑ and walk along the left-hand edge of a field. Just beyond the corner, follow a path through trees to a narrow lane, turn right and after ¼ mile, turn right beside a gate **C** to join the Macmillan Way. Walk along a track through trees, continue along a left-hand field edge and go through a metal gate onto a lane.

Turn left, at a public bridleway sign turn right onto the grass verge to a gate and stile **D**. Turn left alongside a hedge, parallel to the drive to Pinbury Park. After following the curve of the hedge to the left, veer away from it to continue just above the drive. At a small pool, join the drive and keep along it to where it bears right to Pinbury Park. Here continue downhill along a gravelled drive, passing in front of the fine manor house, and to the left is a grand view over the deep and thickly wooded Frome Valley.

The track curves right into trees. Ignoring two paths that branch off to the left, continue down to cross the river at a ford, using a footbridge and a

gate. Keep ahead through another one and head uphill through woodland, eventually emerging from the trees at a fork. Keep right to a metal gate. After going through it, continue along the right-hand edge of two fields and in the corner of the second field – by a group of trees known as the Gloucester Beeches – go through a metal gate and immediately turn right through another gate **E**.

Keep along the right-hand edge of a large field. From this open, elevated position there are fine and extensive views all round, especially looking ahead to Edgeworth Manor and church. Cross a stile by a galvanised gate, head down to two hand gates and descend into a hollow. Make for some stone cottages and turn right onto a tarmac drive to the church **A**. Turn left to retrace your steps up the lane to the start. ●

Miserden and Winstone

		GPS waypoints
Start	Miserden	🖉 SO 937 088
Distance	5 miles (8km)	Ⓐ SO 942 085
Approximate time	2½ hours	Ⓑ SO 947 090
Parking	Roadside parking at Miserden	Ⓒ SO 956 095
Refreshments	Pub at Miserden	Ⓓ SO 963 096
Ordnance Survey maps	Landranger 163 (Cheltenham & Cirencester), Explorer 179 (Gloucester, Cheltenham & Stroud)	Ⓔ SO 961 095
		Ⓕ SO 956 092

The small and secluded villages of Miserden and Winstone occupy opposite sides of the thickly wooded and steep-sided Frome Valley, and this walk links them via field and woodland paths, going through part of Misarden Park. Both villages have interesting churches, and there are fine views across the valley.
There is some strenuous climbing at the start and finish.

The walk starts in the centre of the pleasant village of Miserden, at the octagonal shelter built around a large

Miserden

tree. Nearby is the medieval church – much restored in the Victorian era – and the Carpenters Arms.

🖉 With your back to the pub, take the lane ahead and almost immediately turn right, onto a path. After a few paces branch left by a stone cottage and follow an enclosed path to a stone stile. Climb it, walk along a shady enclosed track and climb another stone stile onto a lane.

Turn left and, where the lane bears right, turn left through a kissing-gate Ⓐ and head downhill across a field. As you descend there are fine views to the left across the Frome Valley, with Miserden Abbey clearly visible. This Jacobean mansion was restored in the 19th century and partly rebuilt by Lutyens in the 1920s following a fire. It is surrounded by fine gardens and parkland, and the gardens are open to the public in the summer on three days a week.

Go through another kissing-gate and

continue downhill along the left, inside edge of woodland to reach a tarmac track. Turn left – still downhill – and at the bottom, turn right onto a track that bears right and continues alongside Misarden Park Lake. Now head uphill through woodland, curving right to join a tarmac drive at a bend and by a blue-waymarked post ⒷB. Walk along this beautiful, tree-lined drive to emerge through gates beside a lodge onto a lane.

Take the narrow lane opposite, turn left at a T-junction, in the Winstone and Birdlip direction, and the lane bends right ⒸC into the scattered village of Winstone. At a fork, take the left-hand, upper lane, signposted to Elkstone and Birdlip, which bends right, keep ahead at a crossroads, and at a public footpath sign turn right onto a tarmac track ⒹD. The track heads gently downhill to a lane, where you turn left for a brief detour to Winstone church, in an isolated and idyllic setting on the eastern edge of the village. This attractive building with a saddleback tower dates back to around the Norman Conquest.

From the church, walk back along the lane back into the village. At a fork take the left-hand, lower lane and, at a public footpath sign, turn left onto a path ⒠E and head down to climb a stile. Walk across a field, go through a gate in the corner, bear right and head diagonally across the next field to climb a stile in the far corner onto a lane. Turn left and at a footpath sign and stone stile turn right along a track ⒡F. The track passes by farm buildings and continues in a straight line across fields, later bending right to keep along the left-hand edge of a field.

In the field corner, follow the track into woodland and, at a waymarked post, bear right and continue through this delightful woodland to merge with another track before reaching a T-junction just to the left of the tarmac drive that was walked along earlier ⒷB. Turn left to rejoin the outward route and retrace your steps to the start, enjoying more grand views over the Frome Valley. ●

Longborough, Sezincote and Bourton-on-the-Hill

Longborough, Sezincote and Bourton-on-the-Hill

		GPS waypoints
Start	Longborough	🥾 SP 178 296
Distance	5½ miles (8.9km)	Ⓐ SP 174 311
Approximate time	2½ hours	Ⓑ SP 174 323
Parking	Roadside parking at Longborough	Ⓒ SP 189 311
Refreshments	Pub at Longborough, pub at Bourton-on-the-Hill	Ⓓ SP 181 297
Ordnance Survey maps	Landrangers 151 (Stratford-upon-Avon) and 163 (Cheltenham & Cirencester), Explorer OL45 (The Cotswolds)	

From Longborough, this undemanding route heads in an almost straight line to Bourton-on-the-Hill, passing close to the impressive and unusual Sezincote House, built in an Oriental style. The return leg takes a more circuitous route across fields. Throughout the walk, there are fine views over the surrounding countryside of the north Cotswolds.

Longborough is a pleasant and unpretentious village with attractive cottages and a medieval church that has a Norman doorway and 13th-century tower. Inside the church there are some interesting monuments.

🥾 The walk starts in the village centre by the war memorial and Coach and Horses. With your back to the pub and facing the church, turn left and, at a public footpath sign to Sezincote and Bourton-on-the-Hill, turn right along a tarmac track, which narrows to a path and leads to a gate.

Go through the gate, walk along the right-hand edge of a field, go through another gate and continue along the right-hand edge of fields. After passing through a belt of trees and through another gate, keep along the left-hand edge of the next field and cross a tarmac drive to a kissing-gate. Go through and walk initially along the left-hand field edge, by woodland on the left, later bearing right and heading downhill towards a lake. Go through a gate at the bottom. As you continue across a field there is a grand view to the left of Sezincote House, built around the beginning of the 19th century for Charles Cockerell, a former employee of the East India Company, in an Indian design. At that time anything Oriental – Indian or Chinese – was highly fashionable. A Moghul palace set amidst landscaped English gardens and with a Cotswold backcloth is a strange sight, but it all seems to blend together beautifully.

Go through a gate Ⓐ across the end of an arm of the lake, go through another gate and continue by the right-hand field edge. At a fence corner, keep straight ahead across the field – crossing a tarmac drive – go through a kissing-gate on the far side, keep ahead to go through another and continue across the next field. The houses and church tower of Bourton-on-the-Hill can be seen ahead. Climb a stile, keep ahead across the next two fields, going through two gates, and then continue along the left-hand edge of the next field to point **B**. Go through another gate and walk along an enclosed path to a lane.

Turn right for a short circuit of Bourton-on-the-Hill. Follow the lane around a left-hand bend to the main road and turn left uphill, passing the mainly 15th-century church. Despite the heavy traffic on the A44, Bourton is still an attractive village with some fine 17th- and 18th-century cottages. Take the first lane on the left, at a T-junction turn left downhill and, at a public footpath sign to Sezincote and Longborough, turn right onto a path and retrace your steps back to the second gate.

After going through it, turn left along the left-hand field edge, go through a gate and keep along the left-hand edge of the next three fields, going through two more gates. On reaching a wide

Countryside near Longborough

hedge gap, turn right, in the direction of a yellow waymark, along an enclosed, hedge-lined path and, at the next way-marked post, turn left at a stile along the left-hand edge of a plantation and climb a stile onto a tarmac drive. Climb the stile opposite, keep along the left-hand field edge, climb a stile in the corner and keep ahead along a narrow path through trees to climb another stile.

Continue along the left-hand edge of the next field and in the corner turn left over a footbridge. Keep by the right-hand field edge to a gate in the corner. Turn right onto a track by a cattle-grid and walk along a tarmac track, going through another gate, towards a farm. Where the track turns right, keep ahead in front of a house and beside a barn to a T-junction. Turn left, go through a gate and continue along a wide, grassy path across fields, curving left to go through a gate at a corner of a wood. Turn right initially along the left-hand edge of the trees, continue across the field but at a crossing of paths about

halfway across – where there is a waymarked tree stump turn right **C**, head across towards the wood again and go through a gate in the field corner.

Walk along the right-hand edge of the next field, looking out for yellow waymarks in the fence on the right where you turn half-left and head across to another waymark on the far side. Turn right to continue along the left-hand field edge, curving left to cross a footbridge, and bear right across the corner of a field to a stile. Climb it, keep in the same direction across the next field towards Longborough church, cross a footbridge over a ditch and bear left diagonally across a field to a stile in the far corner.

Climb the stile, keep along the right-hand field edge but almost immediately turn right over a stile and bear left across the next field towards houses on the edge of Longborough. Climb a stile on the far side, walk along an enclosed tarmac path to a road and keep ahead to a T-junction **D**. Turn right through the village and turn left by the church to return to the start. ●

Somerford Keynes and the River Thames

		GPS waypoints
Start	Cotswold Water Park, Keynes Country Park	🖊 SU 028 959
Distance	6 miles (9.7km)	Ⓐ SU 026 966
Approximate time	3 hours	Ⓑ SU 018 955
		Ⓒ SU 018 947
Parking	Keynes Country Park, near lakeside café	Ⓓ SU 036 941
		Ⓔ SU 028 951
Refreshments	Café at Country Park, pub at Somerford Keynes	
Ordnance Survey maps	Landranger 163 (Cheltenham & Cirencester), Explorer 169 (Cirencester & Swindon)	

This is the second walk in this guide in the Cotswold Water Park. It is a flat and easy route which starts by heading across to the village of Somerford Keynes and then follows a stretch of the Thames Path – at this stage the river is nothing more than a narrow stream. There are many extensive views across the numerous lakes that make up the Water Park and a particularly attractive and relaxing finale along a tree-lined lakeside path.

Keynes Country Park is in the heart of the Cotswold Water Park, an extensive area of lakes in the upper Thames Valley – over 130 and still growing – created from gravel extraction. It has become an established and popular centre for watersports of all kinds, and other outdoor activities: cycling, horse-riding and walking.

🖊 The walk begins by the lakeside café. Turn left along the tarmac drive back towards the entrance to the country park and, at a T-junction, turn right onto a track that keeps along the left-hand edge of a lake. When the path curves right by some seats at the corner of the lake, turn sharp left.

Walk along a path that turns right, continue between a hedge on the left and the embankment of current gravel workings on the right, and climb a stile over to the left in the trees. Follow the path Ⓐ along the left, inside edge of woodland, climb a stile and keep ahead across a field, crossing two more stiles and keeping parallel to its right-hand edge. After crossing a footbridge, keep ahead in the same direction across the next field and climb a stile onto a lane. Cross over, climb the stile opposite, at a public footpath sign to Somerford Keynes, and turn right onto a narrow path that runs through a belt of woodland parallel to the lane. The path bends left – still parallel with the lane – and briefly emerges onto the edge of a field, turning right to a stile.

Climb it to rejoin the lane, turn left and follow the lane into Somerford Keynes. On the edge of the village, turn right along a lane signposted to 'Parish Church' Ⓑ and turn left over a stone

SCALE 1:25000 or 2½ INCHES to 1 MILE 4CM to 1KM

0	200	400	600	800 METRES	1
					KILOMETRES
					MILES
0	200	400	600 YARDS	½	

stile, at a public footpath sign. Walk along an enclosed path, turn right towards the medieval church at a T-junction in front of a wall and bear left through a kissing-gate at a public footpath sign. Head diagonally across a field, cross a footbridge on the far side, walk initially along the right-hand edge of the next field and then continue straight across it. On the far side, turn left along the field edge, here joining the Thames Path, and turn right through a kissing-gate in the corner.

Keep along the right-hand edge of the next field – the infant River Thames

is over to the right – and in the corner, cross a footbridge over the river and turn left onto a tree-lined path, between a lake on the right and the river on the left. Keep along this path and, after emerging from the trees, bear left across to the corner of a meadow to re-enter woodland. Bear left to a road by Neigh Bridge Country Park car park ⓒ. Turn left to cross a bridge over the Thames and, where the road bends left back into Somerford Keynes, turn right along Mill Lane.

Cross a main road, continue along the lane opposite. Pass a residential development and the lane continues as a broad track between lakes. At a Thames Path marker-post in front of gates, turn right to cross a footbridge over the river and follow the path to the left to continue between the river on the left and a lake on the right. This attractive path later continues through woodland, and you keep along it as far as a footbridge and public footpath sign.

Turn left 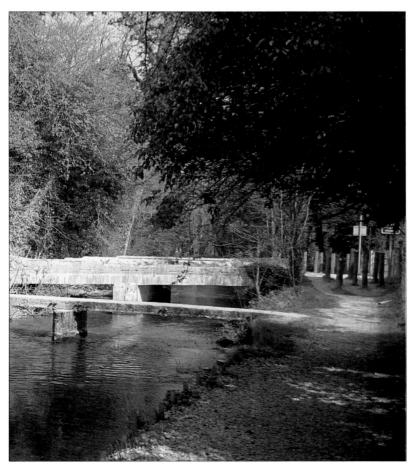 to cross the footbridge over the Thames – here leaving the Thames Path – and follow a path by the right-hand edge of a lake – between trees on the left and a wire fence on the right. On emerging onto a broad track, turn left along a causeway between two lakes, follow the track around a right-hand bend and continue as far as a

The Thames Path in Cotswold Water Park

waymarked post. Turn left here through a hedge gap and turn right to continue along a lakeside path. Keep on it for some time, following it as it bends left. Keep left when the track forks, cross a track and climb a stile in the hedge out to the road. Turn right, follow the roadside path and pass an overhead sign for Keynes Country Park and a stile on the right. Follow the path between a hedge bordering the road on the right and the tree-fringed lake shore on the left. Now comes a most attractive finale to the walk as you follow the path to the left to continue along the lake shore. On emerging into meadowland at the end of the lake, turn left again to return to the start.

Milton under Wychwood and Fifield

		GPS waypoints
Start	Milton under Wychwood	SP 264 183
Distance	6 miles (9.7km)	Ⓐ SP 270 193
Approximate time	3 hours	Ⓑ SP 258 209
Parking	Roadside parking at Milton under Wychwood	Ⓒ SP 254 204
		Ⓓ SP 240 188
Refreshments	Pub at Milton under Wychwood	Ⓔ SP 254 187
Ordnance Survey maps	Landranger 163 (Cheltenham & Cirencester), Explorer OL45 (The Cotswolds)	

Much of the first part of this walk on the western side of the Evenlode Valley is through the beautiful woodlands surrounding Bruern Abbey, parts of which form the Foxholes Nature Reserve. After emerging from the woods, the rest of the route is across more open country, heading up to the small village of Fifield before returning across fields to the start.

The suffix 'under Wychwood' indicates that Milton, along with the neighbouring villages of Shipton and Ascott, was situated beneath the wooded slopes of the medieval royal hunting forest of Wychwood.

Begin at the road junction by the Quart Pot pub and go through a metal gate into a recreation ground. Head straight across the grass and on the far side, just beyond a tennis court, go through a wooden kissing-gate and turn left. Follow the farmland perimeter and, in front of a cottage, turn left through another kissing-gate.

Walk along an enclosed path, cross a footbridge over a brook, keep ahead along a tree-lined path and climb a stile onto a lane. Turn right and after ½ mile, turn left Ⓐ through a gate, at an Oxfordshire Way sign, and walk along an enclosed path. To the right are pleasant views across the Evenlode Valley. Go through a gate, continue along the left-hand field edge and in the corner follow the path into trees. Bear slightly right, and now comes a particularly attractive part of the route as you continue along a broad green ride with a fine view in front of Bruern Abbey, a handsome 18th-century mansion built near the site of a vanished medieval abbey.

At the end of the ride, go through a gate, keep ahead across a field, go through another gate and continue along the left-hand field edge. As you draw level with wrought iron fencing and Bruern Abbey, branch half left to cross an avenue of trees, heading for a gate leading out to the road. Cross it and go through the gate, keeping by the right-hand edge of trees. Pass through a gateway to enter the woodland, part of the Foxholes Nature Reserve. Continue through this delightful woodland, briefly beside the River Evenlode on the right, following the Oxfordshire Way signs to a bridleway sign. Turn left up the track **B**.

Keep left along it, with paddocks over to the right, and go through three gates to enter woodland. Keep along the left edge, following the waymarks and arrows. On reaching a wooden seat and barrier at a crossroads, turn left to the edge of a field **C**.

Turn right here and follow the sometimes overgrown path just inside the woodland. Plunge deeper into the trees, join a track on a bend and when it turns right, go straight on through a gate and along a bridleway. Now head uphill to go through a gate and continue uphill along a track into the small village of Fifield **D**. *Turn left along the lane, bearing right if you wish to see the medieval church, noted for its 14th century octagonal tower topped by a short spire.* Otherwise turn left just before the road bears right and follow a track by cottages. Go through a gate

and head downhill across a field to a stile in its right-hand corner. Go diagonally right in line with telegraph poles, maintain the same direction to a ladder-stile and keep ahead with a stile on the left. Climb a stile and cross the field to the left corner.

Go through the gate, walk diagonally across the next field, aiming for the right-hand side of farm buildings, and go through another gate onto a lane. Turn left and at both bridleway and footpath signs, turn right **E** through a wooden gate and walk along a track.

Where the track ends, go through a gate, walk across a field, cross a brook and keep ahead to go through another gate. Take the path ahead across a field and, on the far side, continue along a track to a road. Turn left into Milton under Wychwood to return to the start. ●

Bruern Abbey

Seven Springs and the Churn Valley

Start	Seven Springs, large lay-by opposite the Seven Springs pub
Distance	6 miles (9.7km)
Approximate time	3 hours
Parking	Lay-by at Seven Springs
Refreshments	Pub at Seven Springs, pub at Cockleford
Ordnance Survey maps	Landranger 163 (Cheltenham & Cirencester), Explorer 179 (Gloucester, Cheltenham & Stroud)

GPS waypoints

- 🖉 SO 967 170
- Ⓐ SO 965 168
- Ⓑ SO 962 159
- Ⓒ SO 964 156
- Ⓓ SO 963 146
- Ⓔ SO 968 140
- Ⓕ SO 975 140
- Ⓖ SO 981 159
- Ⓗ SO 974 165

From Seven Springs, the route takes you through the Churn Valley, passing through the small villages of Coberley and Cowley. After crossing the river, it follows tracks along the eastern side of the valley to return to the start. There are medieval churches in both villages, pubs at the start and approximate halfway point, and fine views over a tranquil landscape.

For long, Seven Springs was considered to be one of the sources of the Thames but it is only the source of the River Churn, one of its many tributaries.

🖉 Facing the pub, turn right along the main road and, at a public footpath sign, turn left through a metal kissing-gate Ⓐ. Walk along the left-hand edge of three fields, climbing several stiles, and later continue gently downhill along an enclosed path into Coberley.

Keep ahead into the village. At the green go straight over to a tarmac path. At the next road cross over to a kissing-gate and join the Gloucesershire Way. Walk down to a footbridge Ⓑ, cross it and veer half left up the bank to a galvanised kissing-gate, leaving the route of the Gloucestershire Way. Cross the field to the next gate and continue across farmland to a junction with a

woodland path Ⓒ. Go through the gate and, with a house and garden on the left, turn right for a few paces to a waymarked junction. Turn left for Cowley, following the clear path between fields. On the far side drop down to a footbridge. Ascend steps, turn right by a wire fence on the left but almost immediately bear right along a faint path through conifers to a gate. Go through and walk along the right-hand edge of farmland. Go through a gate and look for a stile on the right. Climb it, bear left across a field passing along the left-hand edge of a circle of trees. Go through a galvanised gate and continue across the next field, keeping by a wall on the right, to climb another stile. Continue along a track to a lane and keep ahead into the estate village of Cowley. Here there is the classic English combination of great house and church side by side. The former – now a nursing home – is a huge 19th-century mansion and the latter – an attractive medieval church – was heavily restored when the house was built.

In the village, follow the lane around a right-hand bend and take the first turning on the left **D**, signposted to Gloucestershire Guide Headquarters. The lane soon bends left and you keep along it for nearly ¹/₂ mile to a T-junction in front of the Green Dragon Inn at Cockleford. Turn right, take the first lane on the left **E** – signposted 'Cockleford, No Through Road' – and where it bends right in front of a house, turn left through trees and walk along an enclosed path, which descends to cross a footbridge over the River Churn. Keep ahead along a tarmac drive that winds uphill to a road .

Take the uphill tarmac track opposite. After passing farm outbuildings, it continues as a broad, rough track climbing gently between fields, with fine views to the left over the Churn Valley. The track eventually descends to a lane. Turn right, passing by farms, and at a T-junction turn left **G**. Ignore the Gloucestershire Way and bridleway signs, continue along the lane for about $\frac{1}{4}$ mile veering right at the fork. Keep ahead along the track **H**, later descending to a gate. Go through it onto the main road at Seven Springs by a pedestrian crossing. Veer left to the junction and follow the A436 the start.

The Churn Valley

Adlestrop, Evenlode and Chastleton

Adlestrop, Evenlode and Chastleton

Start	Adlestrop	**GPS waypoints**	
Distance	6 miles (9.7km)	🖉 SP 241 271	
Approximate time	3 hours	Ⓐ SP 246 287	
Parking	Adlestrop, village hall car park	Ⓑ SP 225 288	
Refreshments	None	Ⓒ SP 224 291	
Ordnance Survey maps	Landranger 163 (Cheltenham & Cirencester), Explorer OL45 (The Cotswolds)	Ⓓ SP 234 294	

The walk is in the gentle countryside of the Evenlode Valley and there are a series of fine views across the valley. Three quiet and highly attractive villages – all with interesting medieval churches – are passed through and there is an opportunity to visit a fine 17th-century house.

YES, I remember Adlestrop –
The name, because one afternoon
Of heat the express-train drew up
*   there*
Unwontedly. It was late June.

The steam hiss'd. Some one clear'd
*   his throat.*
No one left and no one came
On the bare platform. What I saw
Was Adlestrop – only the name ...

Edward Thomas's poem, written just before the First World War, has immortalised the name of this tiny Cotswold village, as well as vividly evoking the heyday of rural rail travel, when even small and remote villages like this were linked to the outside world without losing their tranquillity or sense of remoteness. Adlestrop could hardly be more perfect: golden stone cottages, many of them thatched, situated close to the great house, which dates mainly from the 16th to the 18th century, and the whole of this gentle

and old-fashioned scene presided over by a medieval church.

🖉 Turn left out of the car park and immediately turn left again along a track. To the right is a small shelter which houses the old station nameplate – placed here, after the station was closed in the 1960s, as a tribute to Edward Thomas, one of the war poets, killed in action in 1917.

After climbing a stile, keep ahead across a field following the Macmillan Way, joining a hedge on the left, and climb a stile in the corner. Walk along a left-hand field edge, climb another stile at a waymarked post and continue along the right-hand edge of the next field. Climb a stile and head gently uphill across a field to a stile on the far side. After climbing it, head uphill through a belt of trees, continue across a field and go through a metal gate in the far right corner Ⓐ.

Turn left, immediately go through a gate and walk along a gently descending, enclosed path called Conygree Lane.

SCALE 1:27 777 or about 2½ INCHES to 1 MILE 3.6CM to 1KM

The route turns left on reaching fields, eventually emerging onto a tarmac drive. Follow this winding drive – which later becomes a lane (Horn Lane) – into the quiet and remote village of Evenlode.

Keep ahead at a junction **B**, keep right at the next junction, follow the lane around a right-hand bend, passing the medieval church, and turn right at the next T-junction.

Pass to the left of a green and at the end of it turn left over a stile, at a public bridleway sign **C**. Walk along the left-hand edge of a series of fields and, in the corner of the fourth and final one, turn left through a gate **D**. Turn right to continue along an attractive, tree-lined track, which eventually ascends to a T-junction. Turn left along a tarmac track that bends right to a lane and turn right.

Just before the lane bends left, the route continues to the right through a gate but just beyond the bend is Chastleton House and church. The house, a fine, unspoilt Jacobean mansion, now owned by the National Trust, was built by a local wool merchant in the early 17th century after purchasing the estate from Robert Catesby, a co-conspirator in the Gunpowder Plot. Inside it has fine panelling and furniture, and its most outstanding features are the Great Hall and the Long Gallery on the top floor, which has a magnificent ceiling. The combination of great house, small village and simple church, which dates back to Norman times, in close proximity could not be more attractive or traditional.

After going through the gate, walk along a track, go through another gate and continue along a tree-lined track. To the right are fine views over the wide Evenlode Valley. On reaching a metal gate **A**, you rejoin the outward route and retrace your steps to the start. ●

Sharpness and Berkeley

		GPS waypoints
Start	Sharpness, picnic site near dock, signposted at end of B4066	SO 667 021
Distance	6½ miles (10.5km)	Ⓐ SO 673 019
Approximate time	3 hours	Ⓑ SO 676 009
Parking	Picnic site at Sharpness	Ⓒ ST 684 998
Refreshments	Pub at Sharpness, pubs at Berkeley	Ⓓ ST 683 989
		Ⓔ ST 672 994
Ordnance Survey maps	Landranger 162 (Gloucester & Forest of Dean), Explorer 167 (Thornbury, Dursley & Yate)	

This walk in the flat countryside adjoining the Severn Estuary begins by following an old track from Sharpness into Berkeley, famed for its medieval castle. It returns to the estuary alongside the meandering Berkeley Pill, and the last mile of the route is beside the river. In such flat terrain the views are extensive, ranging from the Cotswold escarpment in the east to the wooded slopes of the Forest of Dean in the west across the estuary.

The small port of Sharpness grew up where the Gloucester and Sharpness Canal, opened in 1827, empties into the Severn Estuary.

Start by turning right out of the car park along Great Western Road, passing a row of cottages, turn left at a T-junction and, at a crossroads, turn right. Bear left along a tarmac path, at a Severn Way sign, go through a metal kissing-gate and keep ahead across a field.

Go through two more kissing-gates in quick succession, cross a railway line and continue along a tarmac path to a road Ⓐ. There is a pub just to the left. Turn right, at a junction keep ahead along Sanigar Lane and pass under a railway bridge to a T-junction. Turn left, in the Berkeley direction, and after almost ½ mile, turn right onto a tarmac track Ⓑ. The track curves left and continues as a broad, rough, hedge-

lined track for the next mile, eventually heading uphill to emerge onto a road on the edge of Berkeley Ⓒ.

Turn right and follow the road into the Market Place in the centre of the small town. Turn left, almost immediately turn right along High Street and turn left up Church Street to visit Berkeley's three main attractions: Jenner Museum, church and castle. First comes the museum to Dr Edward Jenner (1749–1823), the pioneer of smallpox vaccination. Beyond that is the 13th-century church, with its fine array of lancet windows on the west front. Jenner is buried in the church and there are many tombs and monuments to the Berkeley family.

To gain access to Berkeley Castle, turn left on entering the churchyard – passing by the detached 18th-century bell tower – and just before going under a bridge, turn right up steps to the castle entrance. This grand 12th-century fortress has been the ancestral home of the Berkeleys since the Middle Ages and is perhaps best known for the horrific death of Edward II, murdered here in 1327 on the orders of his wife. The dungeon where this took place can still be seen. The buildings are grouped around the great Norman keep, and

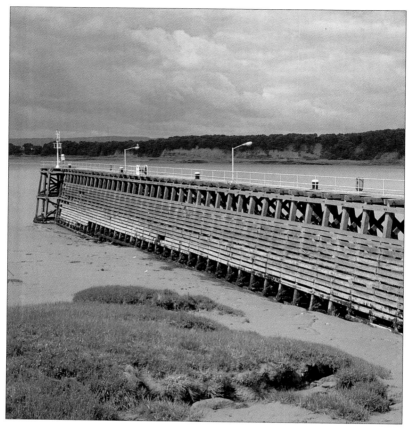

The Severn Estuary at Sharpness

since the castle was largely remodelled in the 14th century, its external appearance has remained largely unchanged. Inside it has been transformed from a bleak medieval castle into a stately home and contains a fine collection of paintings, furniture, tapestries, silver and porcelain. The attractive grounds include an Elizabethan terraced garden.

Return to High Street and turn left *(at this point a brief detour ahead, turning left at a public footpath sign to Woodford into a meadow, rewards you with a fine view of the castle)*. Otherwise, the route continues to the right along Jumpers Lane **D**. Where the lane turns right, keep ahead and walk across grass in front of cottages. Now you keep

above Berkeley Pill, following the meanderings of the stream through several gates to finally reach a kissing-gate leading onto a road to the right of a bridge **E**.

Cross over, climb a stile opposite – here joining the Severn Way – and continue above the winding pill, climbing more stiles. Eventually the path takes you to the top of a broad embankment and, after going through a metal gate, you reach the Severn estuary. The path curves right to keep alongside the river back to the start. Approaching Sharpness, climb a metal stile, turn right along the edge of a grassy area, passing by the end of a row of cottages, and continue along a road. Turn left to return to the picnic site. ●

Deerhurst, Apperley and the River Severn

		GPS waypoints	
Start	Deerhurst, by Odda's Chapel, signposted from B4213	📷	SO 869 298
		Ⓐ	SO 867 291
Distance	7 miles (11.3km)	Ⓑ	SO 866 279
Approximate time	3½ hours	Ⓒ	SO 862 280
Parking	Deerhurst	Ⓓ	SO 862 268
Refreshments	Pub near Mumford's Farm, pub at Haw Bridge, pub on riverside path	Ⓔ	SO 848 262
		Ⓕ	SO 846 278
Ordnance Survey maps	Landrangers 150 (Worcester & The Malverns) and 162 (Gloucester & Forest of Dean), Explorer 179 (Gloucester, Cheltenham & Stroud)		

From Deerhurst, noted for its Saxon church and chapel, the route crosses fields to Apperley and continues by the banks of a disused canal to reach the River Severn. The final three miles (4.8km) is a pleasant and relaxing walk beside the river, following the Severn Way. As this is an almost entirely flat walk, there are wide and extensive views in all directions, eastwards to the line of the Cotswolds and westwards – across the river – to the impressive profile of the Malverns.

Saxon churches are something of a rarity but in the small village of Deerhurst there are two. The walk starts by Odda's Chapel, a small late-Saxon chapel built by Odda, a kinsman of Edward the Confessor, in 1056. Nearby is the church which, although mainly medieval, retains some of its original Saxon stonework, arches and doorways. It was founded as a monastery, probably during the 8th century, and was a place of some importance in Saxon England but declined after the Norman Conquest with the rise of the great abbeys of Evesham, Tewkesbury and Gloucester in the locality. After its suppression in the 15th century, it became a parish church.

📷 Where the lane ends at the car park, turn left over a stile, at a public footpath sign, and walk diagonally across a field in the direction indicated by a yellow arrow. Look out for a stile on the right at the end of a line of trees and head across to climb it. Continue across the next field and climb a stile in the far corner onto a narrow lane.

Turn right, follow the lane around a left-hand bend and at a right-hand bend, keep ahead Ⓐ, passing to the left of a gate, to a stile. Climb it, walk along an enclosed path, by a plantation on the right, keep straight ahead across a field to climb a footbridge on the far side. Keep in the same direction across a playing field to a road, turn right and, at a public footpath sign, turn left over a stile. Continue by a fence either side. Turn left in the field corner, then right at a stile. Walk across the end of a garden and climb another stile. Bear

SCALE 1:25000 or 2½ INCHES to 1 MILE 4CM to 1KM

0	200	400	600	800 METRES	1
					KILOMETRES
					MILES
0	200	400	600 YARDS	½	

slightly left across a field, climb a stile in the far corner, continue in the same direction across the next field and climb a stile onto a road in front of the Farmers Arms **B**.

Turn right and, at a public footpath sign, turn right over a stile and head gently uphill in a straight line between widely spaced trees. In the top, right-hand corner, climb two stiles in quick succession and continue over the brow of a hill to another stile. Climb it, walk across the next field, climb a stile, continue across the next field and climb a stile in the right-hand corner. Walk along a fence-lined path to emerge onto a lane in Apperley Ⓒ. The main part of the village – with its green, pond and brick-built church – is to the right.

Turn left and at a public bridleway sign – where the lane bears right in front of a new housing estate (Moores Ground) – turn left onto an enclosed path. This attractive, tree-lined path descends gently to a road. Cross over and continue along the enclosed track opposite. The track later bends right, turns left in front of a gate and finally crosses a footbridge to a T-junction Ⓓ. Turn right along a path that keeps beside the disused Coome Hill Canal on the left for just over ¾ mile, eventually going through a gate onto a lane. The canal was built in 1796 to link the coalfields of the Forest of Dean with Cheltenham. It closed in 1876, and the area is now a nature reserve.

Turn left along the lane to cross a bridge over the disused canal and after ¼ mile turn right over a stile to join the Severn Way Ⓔ. Walk across a meadow, bearing right to keep parallel with the riverbank, and at its far edge turn first right and then left to climb a stile. Bear left across the next meadow and climb two stiles in quick succession. Now continue along the riverbank to a road, climbing several stiles. In the last field before the road, look out for a stile on the left about halfway along it. Climb the stile, turn right and head across to climb another one and walk along a track, passing to the left of a house. At a fork, take the left-hand path, which heads up to the road to the right of Haw Bridge Ⓕ.

Cross over, climb the stile opposite and continue by the River Severn back to Deerhurst. At one point the route keeps along the edge of a caravan site and passes the Coalhouse Inn but otherwise it is mainly across meadows beside the river, crossing several stiles. Soon after passing the Yew Tree Inn on the opposite side of the river, you reach a public footpath sign in front of a large, solitary oak tree. Turn right along a track and go through a gate to return to the start. ●

The River Severn

Lechlade, Kelmscott and the River Thames

		GPS waypoints
Start	Lechlade	🖊 SU 214 995
Distance	7½ miles (12.1km)	Ⓐ SU 223 991
Approximate time	3½ hours	Ⓑ SU 233 993
Parking	Lechlade	Ⓒ SU 249 993
Refreshments	Pubs and cafés at Lechlade, pub at St John's Bridge, pub at Kelmscott	Ⓓ SU 252 988
		Ⓔ SU 223 989
Ordnance Survey maps	Landranger 163 (Cheltenham & Cirencester), Explorer 170 (Abingdon, Wantage & Vale of White Horse)	

This is an entirely flat walk, which begins by heading across meadows and along lanes into the village of Kelmscott, with its manor house and tiny church. Here you join the Thames Path, and the remainder of the route is along the banks of the meandering river. The final stretch across riverside meadows, between St John's Bridge and Ha'penny Bridge, is especially memorable, with fine views of the tower and spire of Lechlade church.

Lechlade lies on the north bank of the River Thames in the south-east corner of Gloucestershire, near the borders with Oxfordshire and Wiltshire. It is an attractive little town, clustered around its handsome Market Place and dominated by an imposing 15th-century church. The latter, one of the great 'wool churches' of the Cotswolds, has a tower and slender spire visible for miles around across the flat terrain of the upper Thames valley. Inside it is light and spacious with a superb chancel roof. The churchyard inspired some of Shelley's verses, and the opening part of the route is called 'Shelley's Walk'.

The walk begins in the Market Place by the church. Take the paved path to the left of the church, cross a lane, go through a metal kissing-gate and walk along a straight tarmac path. Go through a kissing-gate, keep ahead to go through another one and continue along an attractive, tree-lined path, which emerges

KELMSCOTT CP

onto a road to the left of St John's Bridge Ⓐ. Take the lane opposite and after ¾ mile turn right over a stile Ⓑ at a public footpath sign, and walk diagonally across a field. Climb a stile in the corner, keep along the left-hand edge of the next two fields and, at a hedge corner, continue across the field to cross a footbridge over a brook on the far side. Head straight across the next field towards the far right corner, where you emerge onto a lane at a bend.

Keep ahead to Kelmscott church, a small but interesting building of Norman origin, virtually unaltered since the 16th century. Inside are some medieval wall paintings. The grave of William Morris, 19th-century poet, craftsman and social reformer, who lived at the nearby manor, is in the churchyard. Just beyond the church, turn right along a lane Ⓒ and, after passing the Plough Inn, the lane curves left into the small village. At a T-junction, turn right along a lane which ends by Kelmscott Manor, an Elizabethan house that was the home of William Morris from 1871 until his death in 1896. The house contains many of his possessions, including ceramics, furniture and textiles.

Bear left to continue along a track to the River Thames and turn sharp right, crossing a footbridge and going through a gate, to join the Thames Path Ⓓ. Keep by the river, negotiating several gates, and look out for where a Thames Path sign directs you to turn left to cross a footbridge over an arm of the river. Go through a gate, follow the river round a right-hand bend to another gate to emerge at Buscot Lock. Follow the tarmac path to the right to recross an arm of the river. Do not go through the gate here but continue by the meandering Thames. After going through a metal gate, immediately turn left to cross a footbridge over the river, go through another gate and turn right to continue along the left bank of the Thames. Cross a footbridge over a channel, keep ahead and go through a gate to pass under St John's Bridge **E**. Walk past St John's Lock, go through another gate and follow the Thames across lovely riverside meadows to Ha'penny Bridge.

All the way there are fine views looking upstream to the spire of Lechlade church. After passing under the bridge, turn sharp left up steps to the road. Turn left over the bridge, keep ahead into Lechlade and, at a T-junction, turn right back to the Market Place. ●

Lechlade, dominated by its church spire

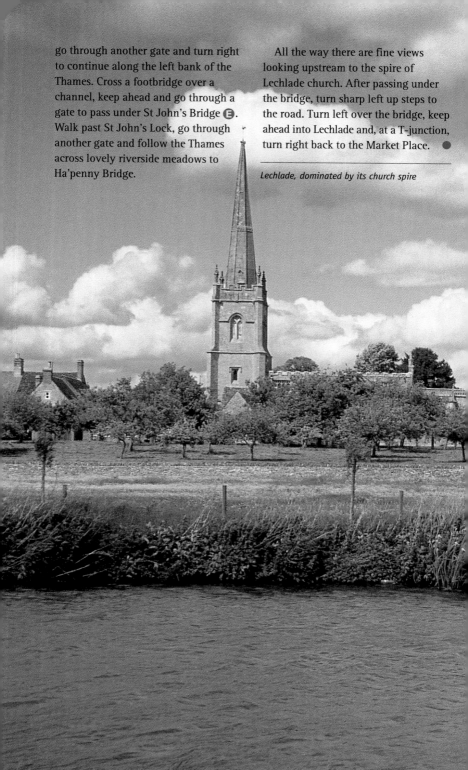

Stow-on-the-Wold, Broadwell and Donnington

		GPS waypoints
Start	Stow-on-the-Wold	📝 SP 191 258
Distance	6 miles (9.7km)	Ⓐ SP 200 268
Approximate time	3 hours	Ⓑ SP 204 274
Parking	Stow-on-the-Wold	Ⓒ SP 192 282
Refreshments	Pubs and cafés at Stow-on-the-Wold, pub at Broadwell	Ⓓ SP 180 279
		Ⓔ SP 174 269
Ordnance Survey maps	Landranger 163 (Cheltenham & Cirencester), Explorer OL45 (The Cotswolds)	Ⓕ SP 180 265

Although there seems to be a high proportion of road-walking on this route, the vast majority of it is along attractive, peaceful and tree-lined lanes. Only the last ³⁄₄ mile into Stow-on-the-Wold is along a fairly busy road and this is made acceptable by a wide verge all the way. In between are quiet tracks and field paths, attractive and unspoilt villages and extensive views over rolling wold country, which together make up a highly enjoyable and interesting walk.

The major route centre of Stow-on-the-Wold lies 755ft (230m) up on the exposed wolds. The focal point of this attractive and popular little town is the large and bustling market square, lined by mainly 17th- and 18th-century buildings and containing a large number of gift and antique shops, inns, restaurants and teashops to cater for the many visitors. In one corner of the square is the medieval church, restored in the 17th century after being damaged while housing Civil War prisoners.

📝 The walk begins in the middle of the market square in front of St Edward's Hall, now the library. With your back to it, turn right across to the corner of the square, walk along High Street and turn right into Parson's Corner. When the road bends sharp right, turn left along a narrow lane, passing some of the town wells, and just after bearing left in front of a house, the lane first becomes an enclosed track and then narrows to a path.

This attractive, tree-lined path emerges onto a lane Ⓐ, and you turn right gently downhill into Broadwell. At a T-junction in front of the spacious green, turn left Ⓑ in the Donnington and Moreton-in-Marsh direction, pass the Fox Inn and, where the lane bends right, keep ahead, at a public footpath sign, along a path to a gate. Go through, continue across grass – later by a wall on the left – and go through a kissing-gate into Broadwell churchyard. The church dates from the 12th century, was enlarged in the 13th, and the tower was built in the 15th century. In the churchyard at the east end of the church is a fine collection of 'wool bale' tombs, so called because they supposedly represent corded bales of wool.

Passing to the left of the church, go through a gate and turn right to a T-junction. Turn left and follow the lane over the A429 and ahead into the hamlet of Donnington. At a fork in front of a barn, take the left-hand lane, turn right at a left bend and, where the lane turns right, keep ahead along a track. Turn left through a waymarked metal gate **C** and walk along the left-edge of farmland. In the second field, when the path splits, keep left to the stone stile and turn half-right across the next field to a waymarked post. Turn left to continue along the right-hand field edge, climb a stile, bear left and head downhill across a field to cross a footbridge over a ditch at the bottom.

Bear right across the next, long field, making for a waymarked stile in the far boundary, and, after climbing it, keep ahead along an enclosed, tree-lined track to emerge onto the A424 **D**.

Take the lane ahead and turn left, in the Upper Swell direction, along a lane that descends, passes by the picturesque Donnington Brewery, crosses the little River Dickler and continues to a road **E**.

Bear left into Upper Swell and, at a Heart of England Way sign and public footpath sign to Lower Swell, turn right through a metal gate. Immediately go through another and continue across two fields, negotiating two stiles. After the second of these, turn left along a narrow, enclosed path to cross a foot-bridge over the River Dickler.

Climb a stile, walk gently uphill along the right-hand field edge, climb over a stile in the corner and go through a wrought-iron gate onto the road **F**.

Turn right, following the road back to Stow-on-the-Wold and at a cross-roads keep ahead along High Street to return to the market square. ●

Donnington Brewery

Painswick and the Beacon

		GPS waypoints
Start	Painswick	🖋 SO 865 096
Distance	6 miles (9.7km)	Ⓐ SO 866 100
Approximate time	3 hours	Ⓑ SO 862 108
Parking	Painswick	Ⓒ SO 856 118
Refreshments	Pubs and cafés at Painswick	Ⓓ SO 865 122
Ordnance Survey maps	Landranger 162 (Gloucester & Forest of Dean), Explorer 179 (Gloucester, Cheltenham & Stroud)	Ⓔ SO 868 120
		Ⓕ SO 867 116
		Ⓖ SO 866 104

From the delightful town of Painswick, the route takes you via field paths, tracks and lanes to the summit of Painswick Hill (Beacon), 928ft (283m) high and a magnificent viewpoint. You then join the Cotswold Way for an easy descent, mainly through woodland, back into the town. Although an undulating walk, none of the ascents or descents are steep or strenuous, and the final climb to the Beacon is relatively undemanding.

In an area of appealing small towns, Painswick must rank among the finest. Occupying a ridge between two valleys, it has a sloping main street, narrow side streets, fine medieval church and a wealth of dignified and attractive houses, all built from creamy-coloured stone. Most of its buildings date from the 17th and 18th centuries, Painswick's heyday as an important centre of the wool trade and cloth-dyeing industry. The church has a 15th-century tower topped by a tall spire, and the churchyard possesses a splendid collection of tombs.

🖋 Turn right out of the car park and walk up the main street, passing the church. Turn left along the B4073, signposted to Gloucester and Upton St Leonards, and where the road curves right, bear left along a lane, Butt Green Ⓐ. At a T-junction, turn right and almost immediately turn left, at a public footpath sign, along a path through trees. Turn left again along a track, go

through a gate and turn right. From here there are pleasant views ahead across the valley, and the 18th-century façade of Painswick House can be seen to the right. The Rococo Garden adjoining this house has been almost fully restored and is open to the public.

Head downhill along the right-hand edge of two fields, climbing two stiles, and continue along a fence-lined path, by woodland on the right. The route continues along the right-hand edge of a field, heading first up and then down, to reach a stile in the field corner. After climbing it, continue gently uphill again along the right-hand edge of the next field and, just over the crest, go through a metal gate onto a tarmac track. Turn right uphill to a T-junction and turn left along a narrow lane Ⓑ.

The lane descends, bends sharply right in front of Holcombe Farm and continues downhill through woodland, passing the handsome Holcombe House.

It then heads uphill and, where the lane curves left at the next farmhouse, bear right ⓒ at a public footpath sign, onto a track and climb a stile. Head diagonally across the field and just to the left of the far right corner, make for a stile and keep ahead along a tree-lined path. Pass the remains of a stile farther up and continue on the enclosed path. Emerging onto a field edge, turn right and follow a track. Keep the hedge on the right and continue on an enclosed track in the field corner. Go through a gate passing in front of the farm buildings, and continue uphill to a lane. Do not turn right along it but take the parallel, straight path, beside the drystone wall, following it along to the B4073. Turn right and at a public footpath sign bear left along a track ⓓ (Wysis Way). At a fork, take the right-hand track towards the Beacon but after about 20 yds turn right off it onto a narrow path that continues uphill, by the right edge of woodland. When you see the triangulation pillar on the summit, turn sharp right and head up to it ⓔ. Painswick Beacon is an area of common land comprising a mixture of open grassland, woodland and disused quarries, and part of it is a golf course. The views from Painswick Hill are magnificent.

Continue along the ridge, bearing right and descending to a path. Turn right and follow it steadily downhill, along the left-hand edge of trees and above a former quarry, to join a broad path. Bear right onto it – the remainder of the walk is along the well-waymarked Cotswold Way – to a lane, turn left and, where the lane bends sharply to the left, turn right along a tarmac track ⓕ. Pass beside a vehicle barrier to a former quarry, now a company called Fire Craft, and in front of the quarry gates take the wooded track to the left. At a fork, take the left-hand path to continue through woodland and, on emerging from the trees, bear right across grass to pick up a path that keeps along the right-hand edge of more woodland.

Keep left on joining a track, continue across part of the golf course, cross a tarmac drive and keep ahead across the course into rough grass on the far side. Follow a path first through the grass and then through trees to a lane and turn right. At a T-junction, turn left ⓖ into Painswick, take the right-hand road at a fork and, where it curves left, pick up the outward route ⓐ to return to the start. ●

Crickley Hill and Leckhampton Hill

		GPS waypoints
Start	Crickley Hill Country Park	🖊 SO 930 163
Distance	7 miles (11.3km)	Ⓐ SO 933 175
Approximate time	3½ hours	Ⓑ SO 945 167
Parking	Crickley Hill Country Park	Ⓒ SO 949 177
Refreshments	Pub near end of the walk	Ⓓ SO 947 176
Ordnance Survey maps	Landranger 163 (Cheltenham & Cirencester), Explorer 179 (Gloucester, Cheltenham & Stroud)	Ⓔ SO 952 185
		Ⓕ SO 939 155
		Ⓖ SO 934 161

Two of the finest vantage points on the Cotswold escarpment, both over 870ft (265m) high, are linked by this walk. There is a varied mixture of wooded and more open terrain, and the views from the two hills, over Cheltenham below and across the Vale of Severn to the line of the Malverns, are magnificent, especially in clear conditions. There is plenty of climbing but all the ascents and descents are easy and gradual.

Crickley Hill Country Park, established in 1979 and comprising a mixture of limestone grassland and woodland, occupies a spur of the Cotswold escarpment. There are superb views, looking across the Vale of Severn to the Malverns on the horizon.

🖊 The first part of the walk is along the Cotswold Way and it starts at the visitor centre. With your back to it, cross a tarmac drive, pass through the car park, go up steps and turn left through a kissing-gate, at a National Trust sign for Crickley Hill. Walk along the ridge and follow a clear, broad path as it bears right to continue through woodland. Go through a gate and bear left to pass a bench. Farther down, the path bears left to a gate. Go down steps and over a stile. Keep by a wire fence on the right, and climb two more stiles to descend to a narrow lane Ⓐ.

Turn right to a crossroads, keep ahead and, where the lane bears right, turn left along an enclosed path Ⓑ, at a public footpath sign to Leckhampton Hill. The path later ascends, continues through trees and finally keeps along a left-hand field edge to a lane Ⓒ. Turn left downhill and, at a Cotswold Way sign, turn right onto an enclosed path Ⓓ, which heads uphill, initially above a disused quarry. Continue uphill across the open grassland of Leckhampton Hill and, at a sign to the Devil's Chimney, make a brief detour to the left to see it. This limestone pinnacle is not a natural phenomenon but was created by 19th-century quarrymen. Much of Cheltenham, seen below, was built from stone quarried here.

Return to the path, turn left and continue over the hill, passing the view-indicator – another outstanding view-point – and curving right to pass to the left of the triangulation pillar on the summit, a height of 961ft (293m). Avoid several gates to reach a junction of paths by a silver birch tree. Turn right **E** and walk along an enclosed path, which bears right to reach a pair of gates, both wooden. Go through either, continue along a straight path through trees to a track and turn left to a lane.

Turn right and, where the lane bears slightly right, turn left onto a path, at a Cotswold Way sign **C**. Here you rejoin the outward route and retrace your steps downhill to where the path emerges onto a lane **B**. Turn left to

leave the outward route and follow the lane to the A436. After crossing it, do not take the lane opposite but bear right along a track that heads steadily uphill and later becomes a tarmac track.

After ¾ mile you reach a metal gate where a track joins from the left. Do not go through it but turn right, at public footpath and Gloucestershire Way signs **F**, to pass beside another metal gate and walk along the left-hand field edge. Bear left through a hedge gap in the corner, bear right and continue across the next two fields. At the wooded corner, go through a gate into woodland. Go through the trees to a gate and down to the A417. Cross over to the Air Balloon pub and turn right to a traffic island. Cross over where the road turns left and follow the Cotswold Way signs ahead. Walk down a track to a gate by a National Trust sign 'The Scrubbs'.

Go through it and, at a three-way fork ahead, take the middle path across grass into woodland. Continue steadily uphill – following the regular blue-waymarked posts – go through a gate at the top and turn left along the drive to the visitor centre.

The Devil's Chimney, above Cheltenham

Brockhampton, Sevenhampton and Whittington

		GPS waypoints	
Start	Whittington village centre		
Distance	5¾ miles (9.2km)	📖	SP 014 209
Approximate time	3 hours	Ⓐ	SP 011 211
Parking	Roadside parking in Whittington	Ⓑ	SP 020 223
		Ⓒ	SP 036 223
Refreshments	Pub at Brockhampton	Ⓓ	SP 033 214
Ordnance Survey maps	Landranger 163 (Cheltenham & Cirencester), Explorer OL45 (The Cotswolds)	Ⓔ	SP 018 207

This walk in the upper Coln Valley links three small, quiet and secluded villages, two of which have interesting and attractive medieval churches and the third a welcoming pub. In between you walk through a typical Cotswold landscape of rolling hills interspersed with stretches of woodland, with a succession of fine views. Expect some of the paths to be muddy and overgrown in places.

📖 Follow the road towards Ham, keeping a telephone box on your right. Continue on the road between trees and bushes and when it turns sharp left for Whalley Farm Ⓐ, go straight on, passing a turning for Whittington Lodge Farm. At the end of the track, go through a gate and continue gently uphill through woodland, going through two more gates. After the second one, you emerge from the wood and keep ahead across grassland – there is a disused quarry on the right – later continuing by a hedge on the left to a metal gate. Go through, keep ahead and at a fork take the right-hand path (blue waymark here), which bears slightly right and keeps by a hedge on the left. The path later becomes tree-lined and continues to a gate.

Go through, walk along the left-hand edge of woodland to a T-junction, turn right to head steadily uphill through the trees, go through a metal gate and continue uphill along the right-hand edge of a field. At a crossing of paths – by a stile on the right – keep ahead alongside a wire fence and continue along its right-hand edge. After passing through a wide gap into the next field, head gently downhill, passing two way-marked posts and continuing down to climb a stile.

Bear slightly left to climb another stile and keep ahead uphill through trees and scrubs to yet another stile. Climb that one, walk along the left-hand field edge, continue uphill through rough grass and finally keep along the left-hand edge of the next two fields, climbing a stile, to finally emerge onto a narrow lane. Turn left, almost immediately turn right **B** in the Winchcombe and Brockhampton direction, and head downhill to a cross-roads by the entrance to Brockhampton Park, a large 19th-century mansion.

Keep ahead, and the lane continues uphill into the village of Brockhampton. About 100 yds before reaching a road junction and small green, turn right **C** along a lane, passing the Craven Arms. Where the lane ends, keep ahead along a narrow path, at a public footpath sign 'Sevenhampton via St Andrews Church', which heads down to a metal gate. Go through to cross the infant River Coln, turn left and walk across a field towards farm buildings. Go through a kissing-gate on the far side, keep by a wall on the right and

go through two kissing-gates into the churchyard. Turn first right and then left to pass to the left of Seven-hampton's delightful church, a narrow cruciform building that dates back to the Norman period and has a Perpen-dicular tower.

Go through a gate onto a lane, go through the kissing-gate opposite, at a public footpath sign to Lower Seven-hampton, and follow a path across a field, bearing slightly left to go through a kissing-gate in the corner. Head downhill to cross a footbridge over the River Coln and keep beside the river to a lane **D**. Turn right to cross a footbridge beside a ford, head uphill beneath a canopy of trees to a T-junction and keep ahead through trees, at a public footpath sign, to a stile.

Climb it, continue uphill along the right-hand field edge, climb a stone stile and keep along the right-hand edge of the next field as far as a the left-hand path signposted Whittington church across the field and climb a stone stile on the far side. Head downhill in the same direction across the next field, climb another stile and continue first through a belt of trees and then along a right field edge. Turn right over a stile and bear left to climb another stile onto a lane **E**.

Cross over, walk along the right-hand edge of a field and follow the field edge to the right to a stile. Climb it, bear slightly left across the next field, making for a kissing-gate on the far side, and go through it onto a lane opposite Whittington Court, a grand 16th-century mansion. Next to it is the tiny Norman church, which has a bellcote instead of a tower. The interior is particularly notable for some fine 14th-century effigies.

Turn right and return to Whittington.   ●

footpath post, where you bear left and head across the field to a ladder-stile. Climb it and keep in the same direction across the next field to a lane. Go straight over to enter a field and at a fork take

Sevenhampton church

Avon Valley

Start	Saltford	
Distance	7 miles (11.3km)	
Approximate time	3½ hours	
Parking	Saltford Picnic Site	
Refreshments	Pub at Saltford, pub at Swineford, pub at Kelston	
Ordnance Survey maps	Landranger 172 (Bristol & Bath), Explorer 155 (Bristol & Bath)	

GPS waypoints

ST 686 673
Ⓐ ST 681 687
Ⓑ ST 690 690
Ⓒ ST 703 691
Ⓓ ST 713 683
Ⓔ ST 700 671
Ⓕ ST 688 672

The area of the Avon Valley covered by this walk lies between Bath and Bristol, and there are distant views of both cities from some of the higher points. Particularly outstanding is the view over Bath from Prospect Stile on the Cotswold Way. Both the climb out of the valley to the village of North Stoke and onto the ridge and the descent back to the river are relatively undemanding. Part of the route uses the Bristol and Bath Railway Path, and there is a short stretch of riverside walking.

Begin by walking along the road, with the River Avon on the right, and at the end of a grassy area, bear right, along a path between bushes. Ascend steps and turn left along the Bristol and Bath Railway Path, the disused track of the former Midland Railway. The railway closed in the early 1970s but was later converted into a tarmac footpath and cycleway between the two cities.

Just after crossing a bridge over the river, turn left down a tarmac path Ⓐ at a sign for the River Avon Trail, turn sharp left to pass under the bridge and continue along the right-hand edge of a succession of fields beside the Avon, finally going through a gate onto a road at Swineford Ⓑ. Take the track opposite, pass through a farmyard and continue along a tarmac track to a picnic site, created on the site of a former iron foundry. At a wall corner – just before reaching the car park – turn right, walk across to climb a stile, head across a field and climb a double stile on the far side. Continue uphill across the next field and pass through a belt of trees to a stile.

After climbing it, keep ahead along a lovely tree-lined path, which continues uphill, winding round to a T-junction. Turn right along a walled track into North Stoke, turn left along an uphill lane and, where it ends, bear left at a public bridleway sign, along a track **C**. Turn right through a metal gate, pass to the left of the restored medieval church up to a stile and gate, climb it and turn right to keep first alongside the churchyard wall. When it ends swing left uphill to a stile and gate, in line with a farm on the right. Continue quite steeply uphill across the next field, making for a waymarked post and continuing past it to a fence corner. Here you join the Cotswold Way and

keep by a fence on the left to a metal kissing-gate.

Go through and follow a grassy path across the middle of Little Down prehistoric fort. At the far end, turn right alongside the earthworks of the fort, keep ahead to a field corner and turn left to continue along the right-hand edge of two fields. In the corner of the second field you reach Prospect Stile **D**, a superb viewpoint over Bath and the Avon Valley, with the Mendips on the horizon. A view-indicator enables you to identify all the places that can be seen in clear conditions.

Go through a kissing-gate, turn left downhill along a narrow path through bushes and the path bends right farther down. Go through a tall kissing-gate

SCALE 1:25000 or 2½ INCHES to 1 MILE 4CM to 1KM

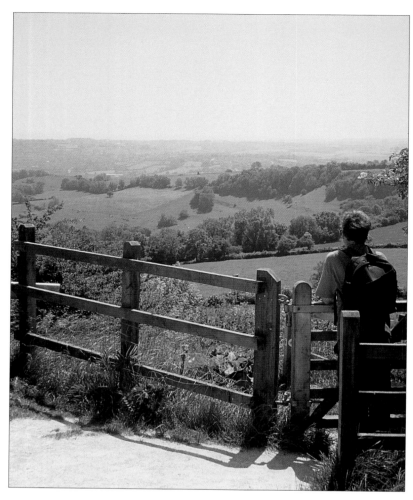

Looking south from Prospect Stile

and continue downhill. In the field corner, turn right onto an enclosed path, take the first turning on the left and continue along another enclosed path. The path descends, goes round several bends and joins a tarmac track by converted barns and outbuildings. Follow it left to the road. Turn left into Kelston and, at a T-junction, turn right **E** along a lane, passing the church over to the left, a medieval building largely rebuilt in 1860.

The lane curves right to a gate, go through and, after a few yards, turn left alongside fencing. Climb a stile on the right, bear left to the next stile, go diagonally across the field to the far corner, turn left through a gate and continue along the left-hand edge of the next field. Go through a gate and bear left along a track to a disused railway bridge **F**.

Turn right over a stile in front of the bridge, immediately turn left up steps, turn left again at the top, turn right and right again to briefly rejoin the Bristol and Bath Railway Path. Just after crossing the River Avon, turn left down steps, here rejoining the outward route, and retrace your steps to the start. ●

Sherborne and Windrush

		GPS waypoints
Start	Sherborne Park, Ewepen Car Park and Information Centre	🖊 SP 159 143
Distance	7½ miles (12.1km)	Ⓐ SP 164 149
Approximate time	3½ hours	Ⓑ SP 177 145
		Ⓒ SP 182 152
Parking	National Trust's Ewepen car park	Ⓓ SP 190 152
Refreshments	None	Ⓔ SP 193 130
		Ⓕ SP 191 134
Ordnance Survey maps	Landranger 163 (Cheltenham & Cirencester), Explorer OL45 (The Cotswolds)	Ⓖ SP 166 140

The first and last parts of this most enjoyable and well-waymarked walk are over the well-wooded slopes of Sherborne Park, which occupies a broad ridge above the valley of Sherborne Brook and from which there are fine views across the valley. In between there is much attractive walking across the lush pastures bordering both Sherborne Brook and the River Windrush, and the route passes through the delightful villages of Sherborne and Windrush.

From the 16th century until 1982, the Sherborne estate was the property of the Dutton family but it is now owned and managed by the National Trust. The Trust has developed an information centre from old farm buildings at Ewepen and has opened up permissive paths across the park, some of which are used on this walk.

🖊 Start by turning right out of the car park along a track and, in front of gates, bear left along a grassy path. The first part of the walk follows a National Trust-waymarked route. Follow the path around a left-hand bend, later descending through trees, and the path then bends right, crosses a small grassy area, curves right again and continues down through woodland.

At a fork, take the left-hand path, which continues winding downhill onto a road Ⓐ. Turn right, passing the entrance to the early 19th-century Sherborne House – now converted into apartments – and church. The latter was mostly rebuilt in the 19th century but retains its medieval tower and spire. Continue on through the attractive estate village to a right-hand bend. Turn left at a sign for Water Meadows Car Park, turn right onto a track Ⓑ and continue along a drive and enclosed grassy path to a gate. After climbing it, turn left along a track and, where it bends right, turn left through a gate and walk diagonally across a field, looking out for a gate to the right of the far corner. Climb it onto a track, turn left, cross a bridge over Sherborne Brook and then bear immediately right to a gate.

Head diagonally across a field, to a gate, keep ahead first along a track and then along a left-hand field edge, by woodland on the left, and go through two gates in quick succession, with a footbridge in between. Turn right along a track **C** that heads gently downhill by a right-hand field edge, continues as an enclosed track and bears right to cross a footbridge over the River Windrush and keep ahead between trees and bushes to emerge into a field.

Turn right onto a broad and undulating track through the valley, following it round first right-hand and then left-hand bends to go through a farmyard, and keep ahead to a metal gate **D**. Do not go through it but turn right along the left-hand field edge, in the corner bear left downhill between trees and bushes, cross a brook and go through a metal gate. Turn left to follow a path across a field, cross a brook, keep in the same direction across the next field and turn right through a metal gate. Keep ahead along a path, curving left to go through a gate, continue curving

The village of Windrush

Retrace your steps along the road through the village and keep along it as far as a track beside a cottage. Turn right, passing to the right of the cottage, head gently downhill and, opposite steps on the right leading up to a stone stile, turn left through a gate **F**. Walk across a field – the River Windrush is over to the right – pass between gate-posts and keep along the left-hand edge of the next three fields. At a wall corner in the third field, veer slightly right and continue across the field to a stile on the far side. After climbing it, again keep along the left-hand edge of the next three fields and, just before the corner of the last field, bear right across to a gate. Go through, walk across the next long field, keeping parallel to its right-hand edge, and go through a gate onto a track.

Go through the gate opposite, here temporarily rejoining the outward route, and retrace your steps to the post office and war memorial in Sherborne village. Leave the outward route here by going through a gate at the corner of the boundary wall of Sherborne Park – there is a National Trust car park sign here – and follow a path into trees. For the rest of the walk there are again regular National Trust-waymarked posts. The path continues along the left-hand edge of woodland, curves left and heads gently uphill by wrought iron fencing. When you reach a bench, where there are views across farmland to Home Farm, bear right into the trees and keep straight on at the junction. Follow the path to the left and on reaching a yew tree with a circular seat walk just beyond it and turn right at the T-junction. Keep to the right of an ice house, make for a wrought iron gate on the left and go through it into the trees. At the next metal gate turn right **G** along a track and follow it to the start. ●

left and climb a stile by Windrush Mill. Turn right around the end of the mill building, follow a path to the left and climb a stone stile.

Turn right uphill alongside a wall on the right, climb a stile, keep ahead by a wall on the left and climb another stone stile. Continue along an enclosed path, which first descends and then heads uphill, becomes a tarmac drive and emerges onto a road in the village of Windrush. Turn left to the church **E**, a particularly interesting building with a superb Norman south doorway, beautiful 15th-century nave roof and imposing Perpendicular tower, which overlooks the small, triangular village green.

Macaroni Downs and the Leach Valley

		GPS waypoints
Start	Eastleach Turville, by the Victoria Inn	🖉 SP 198 052
Distance	7½ miles (12.1km)	Ⓐ SP 191 069
Approximate time	4 hours	Ⓑ SP 189 074
		Ⓒ SP 199 082
Parking	Roadside parking in Eastleach Turville	Ⓓ SP 208 056
Refreshments	Pub at Eastleach Turville	
Ordnance Survey maps	Landranger 163 (Cheltenham & Cirencester), Explorer OL45 (The Cotswolds)	

The opening and closing stretches of the walk are through the lovely Leach Valley, following the elusive and sometimes disappearing small river above the twin villages of Eastleach Turville and Eastleach Martin. In between there is a circuit of the open downland above the valley, returning to the river through woodland. This is a walk in one of the quieter, less-frequented parts of the Cotswolds but has all the classic ingredients of the typical Cotswold landscape: river, woodland, open wold, extensive views and two idyllic villages with fine medieval churches.

Although only divided by the tiny River Leach, Eastleach Turville and Eastleach Martin are separate small villages, each with its own church, which face each other across the river at a distance of no more than 200 yds.

🖉 Start in front of the Victoria Inn and, facing the pub, turn right along an enclosed tarmac path. At a public footpath sign by a cottage, turn left over a stone stile, walk along an enclosed tarmac path to a lane, turn right and take the first turning on the left. Where the lane ends, go through a metal gate and bear slightly right across a field.

After about 50 yds, bear left and continue across the field to go through a metal gate in the far left corner. Walk along a track, by a wall and fence on the left, descend gently to go through a metal gate and continue downhill into the valley. Go through another metal gate to the left of a footbridge over the River Leach and keep ahead along the lower slopes of the valley, going through a metal gate and following the curve of the river to eventually emerge onto a lane via another metal gate Ⓐ.

Turn right over Sheep Bridge, turn left to go through a gate beside a cattle-grid and immediately turn right and head uphill along the left-hand edge of woodland. Climb a stile at the top, keep ahead but at the corner of the woodland head downhill across the grassy slopes to meet a tarmac track by the edge of woodland **B**. Cross it – by a footpath post – and take the track opposite, which ascends gently to a metal gate.

Go through the gate, keep ahead along the right-hand field edge over the Macaroni Downs and go through a metal gate to a crossroads. To the right is a dew pond, thought to date from 1789, and just ahead is a barn. Keep ahead past the barn along the right-hand field edge, go through a gate, continue along the right-hand edge of the next field and bear right to go

through another gate. Walk along the left-hand edge of a field, by woodland on the left, and the track bears right to continue along the left edge. Bear left through a gate to a junction, turn sharp right along a short stretch of hedge-lined track, go through a gate, and head diagonally across a large field to a waymarked post on the far side.

Continue along the left-hand field

edge, pass through a hedge gap to descend to a bridleway post, and bear right to go through a gate. Keep in a straight line along the right-hand edge of several fields, later continuing along an enclosed track, which later still becomes a tarmac lane. Continue along the lane and, at a public bridleway sign, turn right **C** onto a path that keeps along the left-hand edge of woodland. At the corner of the wood, keep straight ahead across a field and on the far side go through a gate onto a lane.

Go through the metal gate opposite and walk along the right-hand edge of a field, by woodland on the right again. At a gap in the trees, turn right onto a track and immediately turn left to continue along a path through the trees. Keep ahead at a crossing and eventually the path joins and keeps by the little River Leach, a delightful part of the walk.

After exiting from the trees via a metal gate, do not keep ahead beside the river but bear slightly left across the field to a stile. Climb it, and go straight across the field to a gate. Continue along the perimeter for about 120 yds to a stile in the right-hand fence. Cross it and turn left, keeping the fence on

your left. Keep above the river and meadows to a metal gate. Keep right, still above the river, finally going through a metal gate onto a lane **D**.

Turn right and follow the lane to a road junction by a small triangular green in front of the medieval church at Eastleach Martin, noted for its Norman doorway and fine 14th-century north transept. The saddleback tower of the mainly 13th-century church at Eastleach Turville on the other side of the river can be seen to the right and involves just a minor detour from the route.

At the junction by the church, keep ahead along the lane signposted to Southrop and Lechlade and, at a public footpath sign, turn right through a gate into the churchyard. Keep to the left of the church, go through another gate, turn left onto a paved path beside the river and turn right to cross a stone footbridge over the river into Eastleach Turville.

This is Keble Bridge, named after the Keble family, who were the local lords of the manor.

Turn left along a lane and follow it as it bears right through the village to return to the starting point.

Eastleach Turville

Cirencester and the Duntisbourne Valley

		GPS waypoints	
Start	Cirencester	🖉	SP 023 020
Distance	8½ miles (13.7km). Shorter version 6 miles (9.7km)	Ⓐ	SP 016 030
		Ⓑ	SP 013 033
Approximate time	4½ hours (3 hours for shorter walk)	Ⓒ	SP 009 040
		Ⓓ	SO 995 046
Parking	Cirencester	Ⓔ	SO 991 053
Refreshments	Pubs and cafés at Cirencester	Ⓕ	SO 985 060
		Ⓖ	SO 994 028
Ordnance Survey maps	Landranger 163 (Cheltenham & Cirencester), Explorers 168 (Stroud, Tetbury & Malmesbury) and 169 (Cirencester & Swindon)	Ⓗ	SP 006 035

From the centre of Cirencester, the walk leads across fields to Stratton and then on through the Duntisbourne Valley to Daglingworth. It continues through the valley to the idyllic hamlet of Duntisbourne Rouse before returning to Daglingworth and taking a different route back to the start. The shorter version omits the extension between Daglingworth and Duntisbourne Rouse. This is a mainly flat walk that encompasses lovely old villages, fine churches and extensive views across rolling country. Leave plenty of time to explore Cirencester, a particularly attractive and interesting old town.

Cirencester reveals little of its illustrious past as one of the foremost towns of Roman Britain (Corinium) and the seat of a great medieval monastery. Apart from a few feet of wall, plus the remains of an amphitheatre to the south of the town, there is nothing to see of Roman Cirencester, except for the numerous artefacts – including some splendid mosaics – in the excellent Corinium Museum. Also, there is virtually nothing left of the abbey, except for one gateway and the site, which is now an attractive park.

What there is to see is one of the grandest of Cotswold 'wool churches'

and some streets of fine old buildings dating from the Middle Ages, when Cirencester developed into one of the principal centres of the wool trade. The church is magnificent: its spacious interior is almost cathedral-like and the superb Perpendicular tower rises to a height of 162ft (49m). Particularly outstanding is the 15th-century, three-storeyed south porch, which overlooks the Market Place.

🖉 The walk starts in the Market Place. Take the paved path that passes in front of the church and continue in a straight line along first Gosditch Street, then Dollar Street, and finally

SCALE 1:25000 or 2½ INCHES to 1 MILE 4CM to 1KM

Gloucester Street – passing a series of attractive old buildings – to join the A435. Walk along the main road to where it forks and turn left, at a public footpath sign, onto a path **A**. Almost immediately turn right through a kissing-gate, walk across a field and go through a wall gap on the far side.

Keep ahead along a track, passing in front of houses and bungalows, cross a lane **B** go through a gate opposite and continue along an enclosed path. Go through a gate, walk along a left-hand field edge, go through a metal gate, continue along an enclosed path, cross a tarmac drive and keep ahead to go through another gate onto a track. Go through the kissing-gate opposite, continue initially by a wall on the right and then head across the field to go through another kissing-gate onto a tarmac drive.

Ahead is Stratton's small church, of Norman origin but largely rebuilt in 1850. After entering the churchyard, follow a slabbed path to the left of the church and head up to a lane. Turn left and, at a public footpath sign to Daglingworth, turn left over a stile **C**, walk along the left-hand edge of a small tree nursery, cross a tarmac drive and turn right through a waymarked gate. Technically, the way continues beside the little Duntisbourne stream but this is physically difficult because of overgrown scrub. Instead, walk along a path and, at the corner of the scrub by a post, turn right down to the stream and turn left to continue beside it along the right-hand edge of a field to a stile.

Climb the stile, walk along the right-hand field edge, following it as it bears right, to a metal gate. Head diagonally across the next field, making for a waymarked post on the far side, and

The idyllic-looking hamlet of Duntisbourne Rouse

lovely view ahead over the valley to the idyllic village of Duntisbourne Rouse. Head downhill towards the village, go through a gate, turn left along a track and cross a footbridge over the stream by a ford. At a public footpath sign, turn right up steps, go through a gate, walk along an enclosed path and go through another gate into the church-yard **F**. The largely Norman church has a low saddleback tower at the west end, and the interior, delightfully simple and unspoilt, retains some medieval wall-paintings. So steep is the slope on which the church is built that there is a crypt at the east end.

From here, retrace your steps to Daglingworth and on past the church to where the route emerges onto a lane at Lower End. Just after joining the lane, turn right **D** at a public bridleway sign, to a broad track and double gates, here rejoining the shorter walk. Follow this gently undulating track across fields for the next $1\frac{1}{4}$ miles to the edge of Cirencester Park, a huge expanse of parkland that extends to the town centre of Cirencester. Do not enter the park but turn sharp left, at a public footpath sign, onto another track **G**.

After $\frac{3}{4}$ mile you reach a crossing of paths where you turn right **H** along a track that keeps along the right-hand edge of a field, by a hedge on the right. Follow the path as it bends left across the field to a gate and continue along an enclosed path, which later becomes a tarmac track. Keep along it into Stratton and, at a public footpath sign, turn right along a track **B**. Here you rejoin the outward route and retrace your steps to the starting point. ●

bear right to keep along the left-hand field edge to a gate. Go through, continue across the next field towards farm buildings, climb a stile in the far right corner and bear left along a track between the farm buildings to a lane at Lower End **D**.

Turn left along a track here, at a public bridleway sign, for the shorter walk.

For the full walk, keep ahead and, where the lane turns right, go through a gate, walk along the right-hand field edge and go through another gate onto a track. Keep ahead, passing to the left of Daglingworth's medieval church, and bear right down into the village. At a crossroads turn left, follow the lane around a left-hand bend and take the first turning on the right, signposted 'The Duntisbournes'. Where the lane curves left, turn right **E** along a narrow lane that heads uphill and peters out into a rough track.

At this point, bear left onto a path, at a public bridleway sign which continues up, passing behind cottages, to a gate. Go through, walk along the left-hand edge of two fields, by woodland on the left, and after going through a gate in the corner of the second field, there is a

Banbury, Oxford Canal and Broughton

		GPS waypoints	
Start	Banbury, the Cross	🖊	SP 453 403
Distance	10 miles (16km)	Ⓐ	SP 460 406
Approximate time	4½ hours	Ⓑ	SP 473 387
Parking	Banbury	Ⓒ	SP 460 383
Refreshments	Pubs and cafés at Banbury, pubs	Ⓓ	SP 444 390
	at Bodicote, pub at Broughton	Ⓔ	SP 430 392
Ordnance Survey maps	Landranger 151 (Stratford-upon-	Ⓕ	SP 420 382
	Avon), Explorer 191 (Banbury,	Ⓖ	SP 430 382
	Bicester & Chipping Norton)	Ⓗ	SP 438 390

From the busy town centre of Banbury, the towpath of the Oxford Canal provides a quick and easy 'green corridor' into quiet countryside. The route continues along an ancient trackway – the Salt Way – and across fields to Broughton. After a brief incursion into Broughton Park, mainly for the classic view of the adjacent church and castle, the Salt Way is used again on the return leg before heading back to Banbury Cross.

Despite recent expansion and modern-isation, the narrow streets and alleys and the many fine old buildings – dating from the 15th to the 19th century – in the centre of Banbury are evidence of its past as a flourishing market town and important route centre. The walk starts at Banbury Cross, of nursery rhyme fame, which is a 19th-century replacement. Nearby is the large and imposing Georgian church, built in 1790.

🖊 Begin by turning down High Street (signposted museum and bus station), at a fork continue along the left-hand street, passing to the right of the town hall, and keep ahead along Bridge Street. Cross the canal bridge but, before reaching the railway bridge, turn left onto a tarmac path Ⓐ signposted Oxford Canal (North) that bends left across a grassy area and at a fork take the left-hand path to the canal.

Turn left onto the towpath of the Oxford Canal, opened in 1790 to link Oxford with Coventry and the industrial Midlands. From the start it was a great commercial success but declined after the coming of the railways. Keep by the canal for the next 1½ miles as far as a brick-built bridge. The noise and bustle of the town is soon left behind as the canal proceeds through tranquil and pleasant countryside. At the bridge, go up steps and over a stile to the left of it and turn right to cross it Ⓑ. This part of the route is waymarked 'Banbury Fringe Circular Walk'. Follow a track gently uphill, keep ahead to emerge onto a road at Bodicote and take the road ahead (Broad Gap) to a T-junction. The village centre, with its old church – mostly rebuilt in 1844 – and thatched cottages, is to the left but the route continues to the right.

Just before reaching a traffic island, turn left along a tree-lined track **C**. This is the Salt Way, part of an ancient route that ran from Droitwich, where the salt was produced, to the River Thames and on to London. Initially the track keeps along the edge of houses on the outskirts of Banbury and continues to a road **D**. Cross over, walk along the hedge- and tree-lined path opposite,

passing below Crouch Hill – the highest point in the vicinity – seen through the trees on the right. Keep to the path and eventually it bends right to reach the road **E**. Cross over to the cycle trail, cross a footbridge and turn left to follow a path parallel to the road. Rejoin it, turn right and then right again at the turning for Newington. Pass the entrance to the Mill House and just beyond it, where the road bends right, go straight on along a lane. On reaching a right of way crossing the road, veer left and follow the Macmillan Way across the fields. Cross a track and head towards Broughton. At the next road cross over to a stone stile and immediately beyond it are two rights of way. Take the left-hand one, pass a stone lodge and head out across parkland. When you draw level with a bend in the drive down to the left, swing left to join it and walk ahead to Broughton church. Ahead is a splendid view of the moated castle. Go through the churchyard and follow the paved

path on the far side. Walk ahead to the road and turn left **F**. At the Saye and Sele Arms, turn right for Bodicote. Go straight on at the road junction and walk along the road. On reaching wrought iron gates on the right, turn left into a field **G** and follow its right-hand boundary. Seventy-five yards before the corner turn right through a gate and keep ahead. On reaching a gap in the hedge, level with Crouch Farm, turn left and then immediately right to a gate. Turn left in the field, keep to the left edge and cross a concrete track. Make for a stile **H** and follow the path across the pasture towards woodland, heading for a telegraph pole. Cross a footbridge and turn right onto the Salt Way, rejoining the outward route to a road **D**. Turn left and follow it into the centre of Banbury, turning left at a T-junction to return to Banbury Cross.

The Oxford Canal near Banbury

Tetbury and Westonbirt

Start	Tetbury	
Distance	9½ miles (15.3km)	
Approximate time	4½ hours	
Parking	Tetbury	
Refreshments	Pubs and cafés at Tetbury	
Ordnance Survey maps	Landrangers 162 (Gloucester & Forest of Dean) and 163 (Cheltenham & Cirencester), Explorer 168 (Stroud, Tetbury & Malmesbury)	

GPS waypoints

- 🖊 ST 891 931
- Ⓐ ST 893 929
- Ⓑ ST 887 907
- Ⓒ ST 882 895
- Ⓓ ST 872 893
- Ⓔ ST 855 894
- Ⓕ ST 844 901
- Ⓖ ST 860 906
- Ⓗ ST 886 927

Although a lengthy walk, it is relatively undemanding as it is across the almost flat terrain bordering the southern Cotswolds that lies to the south and west of Tetbury. The route passes by the imposing Westonbirt House – now a school – and at the approximate halfway point, it takes you across part of Westonbirt Arboretum. It is well worth paying the entrance fee for a fuller look at this vast and superb collection of trees. For much of the way, the slender spire of Tetbury church is in sight.

Even by Cotswold standards, Tetbury is an outstandingly attractive town with a wealth of 17th- and 18th-century houses, built at the time when it was the centre for the local wool trade. The church is unusual in that, although dating from the late 18th century, it is built in the Gothic rather than the contemporary Georgian style. Its tall, slender spire is a landmark for miles around and it has a light and spacious interior. The walk starts in the market square by the 17th-century Market House.

🖊 Facing the Market House and with your back to the Snooty Fox Hotel, turn left and then right along Silver Street. The road curves left downhill and, after crossing the bridge over the infant River Avon, turn right Ⓐ along a tarmac track, at a restricted byway sign. In front of a gate, turn right through a metal gate, bear left and

climb to a stile.

Head uphill to enter a field, turn left and walk along the left-hand edge of the next three fields, climbing a succession of stiles. The route then continues along the right-hand edge of a field and, in the corner, turn right through a gate and walk across a narrow field to another gate. After going through that one, keep ahead across a field, to the next stile and gate and continue to the next gate. Go through, keep ahead, passing between redundant gateposts, and in the next field, look out for where you turn left to cross a footbridge over the stream that you have been following for some time. Head uphill along the right-hand field edge, cross a stile, continue along a wide path beside plantations and, at a public footpath sign, turn right to follow a track along the right-hand field edge and through a gate onto a lane **B**.

Turn right and, at a public bridleway sign, turn left onto a track and follow this delightful tree-lined track (Wormwell Lane) to a lane. Take the lane opposite, signposted to Easton Grey, and at a public footpath sign turn right onto a track **C** and immediately climb a stile. Keep by the left-hand field edge, veering slightly right to go through a gate, and continue across the next two fields. Climb a stile in the corner of the second field, bear left through a gate and walk along a track, to the right of farm buildings. Beyond them look for a track on the left, following it along the gate, and walk along the left-hand field edge.

Go through a gate, follow the track around left- and right-hand bends and continue, by a fence on the left, to go through another gate. Bear slightly right across a field, skirting the left-hand corner of woodland, and continue across to climb a stile on the far side onto a lane **D**. Climb the stone stile opposite, walk across a field to a way-marked gate, go through and keep in the same direction across the next two fields. After going through a kissing-gate on the far side of the second field, continue across parkland, aiming for a waymarked gate on the far side. Over to the right is an impressive view of the grand, 19th-century mansion of

SCALE 1:25000 or 2½ INCHES to 1 MILE 4CM to 1KM

The Market House at Tetbury

Westonbirt House, now a school.

Go through the gate, bear slightly right across the next field, climb a stile and bear right across the corner of a golf course to a tarmac track. Bear left along it to emerge onto a lane and keep ahead through Westonbirt village. At a crossroads, keep ahead to the A433 **E** cross over and take the enclosed, tree-lined path opposite through Westonbirt Arboretum. This magnificent collection of trees and shrubs of all kinds – over 18,000 – was started in 1829 and is being added to all the time. It looks spectacular and is worth a lengthy visit at any season of the year. There is a visitor centre, plant centre, gift shop and café, and an admission charge is payable at the entrance.

The path emerges onto a tarmac track. Keep ahead to a T-junction of tracks, go through a gate with a 'No Parking' sign on it and continue along the right edge of Silk Wood. Cross a track, continue along the edge of the wood to a waymarked post by a stile **F**, turn right keeping left at a fork and head uphill to a gate in the field corner. After going through it, walk along the right-hand edge of a series of fields and through a succession of gates – by the left-hand edge of the arboretum all the while – eventually climbing a stile at the corner of the woodland. Keep ahead, by a wall on the left, and climb a stile onto a lane **G**.

Go through the gate opposite, at a public bridleway sign, and walk along a hedge-lined track, going through two more gates. Continue along a left-hand field edge and look out for where you turn left over a stile. Head gently uphill across a field, climb a stone stile and continue in the same direction across the next field to climb another stone stile in the corner. Bear right along a grassy track – between a fence on the left and a hedge on the right – pass through a wall gap and continue along the right-hand field edge to a stone stile. Climb it, keep ahead across two fields, climbing a stile and crossing the drive to Elmestree House – seen on the left – to a gate to the left of some trees.

After going through two gates in quick succession, walk across a field in the direction of a house, go through a gate on the far side, continue across the next field to join a track in the far corner and go through a gate. Keep ahead, passing to the right of a lodge, go through another gate and continue along a narrow, hedge- and tree-lined lane into Tetbury. Over to the right lies Highgrove, country home of HRH the Prince of Wales. At a T-junction, turn right **H** to the main road and turn left, passing the church, to return to the Market Place. ●

Dursley, Uley and Owlpen

		GPS waypoints	
Start	Dursley	🥾	ST 756 981
Distance	8½ miles (13.7km)	**A**	ST 771 988
Approximate time	4½ hours	**B**	ST 780 993
Parking	Dursley	**C**	ST 786 993
Refreshments	Pubs and cafés at Dursley, pub at	**D**	ST 792 986
	Uley, pub at Woodmancote	**E**	ST 798 983
Ordnance Survey maps	Landranger 162 (Gloucester &	**F**	ST 786 978
	Forest of Dean), Explorer 167	**G**	ST 779 972
	(Thornbury, Dursley & Yate)	**H**	ST 774 974
		J	ST 762 971

There are plenty of 'ups and downs' – some of them steep – on this lengthy, varied and quite energetic walk, especially on the first part as you follow the Cotswold Way along the escarpment from Dursley, over Peaked Down and Cam Long Down. After descending into Uley, the route follows a quiet lane into the secluded hamlet of Owlpen. The rest of the walk is beside the little River Ewelme and along the edge of woodland, before returning to the centre of Dursley through the town's outskirts.

Dursley lies below the well-wooded Cotswold escarpment on the edge of the Vale of Berkeley. The town is centred on the dignified 18th-century Market House and imposing medieval church. The tower of the latter had to be rebuilt in the early 18th century after the collapse of its predecessor.

🥾 The walk starts by the Market House. Turn down Long Street and, where the road bends left, bear half right, following the Cotswold Way. Go through trees and then follow the trail at the sign for Cam Long Down, crossing several fields. The Cotswold Way is well signposted along this stretch. Pass beside a stream on the right and continue with a road on the left. On reaching it, cross over **A** and continue on the Cotswold Way, climbing up the hillside. Make for a

kissing-gate in the top right corner and turn right. Keep left after a few paces, climbing the bank to a junction of paths. Turn right and continue on the Cotswold Way, over the top of Cam Long Down (722ft/220m), a magnificent ridge walk with extensive views on both sides and ahead. At the end of the ridge, descend steeply through woodland, following a winding, path down to a stile. After climbing it, descend towards a farm below. Keep along the left-hand edge of the next field, climb a stile and continue along a narrow lane **B**.

Where the lane turns right, turn left along a track, at a public bridleway sign, which bears right and heads uphill, passing between farms. It then continues steeply uphill through trees to pass beside a gate onto a road. Just before the road, turn right **C** beside a wooden gate, at a public bridleway sign, along a broad, tree-lined track and, on emerging from the trees, turn left onto a path that keeps by the earthworks of Uley Bury, the site of a prehistoric settlement now covered by crops.

Look out for a fork where you take the left-hand, lower path, which descends quite steeply to enter woodland. Continue down through this delightful woodland, passing a bridleway on the left, and the path winds down to a gate. Go through and continue downhill along the top edge of a sloping field, bearing right away from the field edge to a kissing-gate. Go through, keep ahead along an enclosed path and turn left alongside the churchyard wall at Uley to a road. The church is a fine Victorian building but the 18th-century houses in this

now quiet village are a reflection of its heyday as a busy centre of cloth production.

Turn left and, by the Old Crown pub, bear right along Fiery Lane **D**, sign-posted to Owlpen, and follow it for $^1/_2$ mile into the secluded hamlet. Here the lane curves right to pass by the Tudor manor-house and below the 19th-century church, a delightful combination lying at the foot of a wooded hillside and above the little River Ewelme. At a public footpath sign, turn right over a stile **E** – the stile ahead not the one on the right – and continue across a series of meadows and over a succession of stiles, by the River Ewelme on the right. In the tapering corner of the last meadow, cross a footbridge over a brook, head uphill and continue across more fields and through a succession of kissing-gates, finally climbing a stile in the last field corner onto an enclosed path.

Keep along the path, over a track and on through trees, to a road, turn right and take the first lane on the left, signposted to Shadwell and Elcombe **F**. The lane bends right and, where it curves left, bear right, at a public footpath sign, along a tree-lined track. Keep to the left of several houses, bear right to climb a stile and walk diagonally across two fields to the far right corner. Do not climb the stile there but turn left along the field edge, by a fence on the right, cross a stile and follow the field edge to the left and climb a stile in the corner.

Immediately climb another one, keep ahead by the right-hand field edge, turn right over a stile, bear left across the corner of the next field and go through a gate. Head gently uphill along the right-hand edge of the next field and climb a stile onto a track. Turn right, avoid the immediate track and then veer left at a footpath sign **G**.

Cross the fields with woodland over to the left, cross the next stile and then keep going on the track. After the next stile, continue for about 100 yds, then turn right into the adjoining field. Go diagonally left, keeping Sheephouse Farm on the right. Cross two stiles, avoid a drive running off to the right and keep along the field edge **H**. Make for a galvanised gate and stile and continue on an enclosed path to merge with a track. Turn right at the road **J** and follow it through Woodmancote. Bear left at the next main junction and return to Dursley town centre.

Further Information

 ### The National Trust

Anyone who likes visiting places of natural beauty and/or historic interest has cause to be grateful to the National Trust. Without it, many such places would probably have vanished by now.

It was in response to the pressures on the countryside posed by the relentless march of Victorian industrialisation that the trust was set up in 1895. Its founders, inspired by the common goals of protecting and conserving Britain's national heritage and widening public access to it, were Sir Robert Hunter, Octavia Hill and Canon Rawnsley: respectively a solicitor, a social reformer and a clergyman. The latter was particularly influential. As a canon of Carlisle Cathedral and vicar of Crosthwaite (near Keswick), he was concerned about threats to the Lake District and had already been active in protecting footpaths and promoting public access to open country-side. After the flooding of Thirlmere in 1879 to create a large reservoir, he became increasingly convinced that the only effective way to guarantee protection was outright ownership of land.

The purpose of the National Trust is to preserve areas of natural beauty and sites of historic interest by acquisition, holding them in trust for the nation and making them available for public access and enjoyment. Some of its properties have been acquired through purchase, but many have been donated. Nowadays it is not only one of the biggest landowners in the country, but also one of the most active conservation charities, protecting 581,113 acres (253,176 ha) of land, including 555 miles (892km) of coastline, and more than 300 historic properties in England, Wales and Northern Ireland. (There is a separate National Trust for Scotland, which was set up in 1931.)

Furthermore, once a piece of land has come under National Trust ownership, it is difficult for its status to be altered. As a result of parliamentary legislation in 1907, the Trust was given the right to declare its property inalienable, so ensuring that in any subsequent dispute it can appeal directly to parliament.

As it works towards its dual aims of conserving areas of attractive countryside and encouraging greater public access (not easy to reconcile in this age of mass tourism), the Trust provides an excellent service for walkers by creating new concessionary paths and waymarked trails, maintaining stiles and footbridges and combating the ever-increasing problem of footpath erosion.

For details of membership, contact the National Trust at the address on page 95.

 ### The Ramblers' Association

No organisation works more actively to protect and extend the rights and interests of walkers in the countryside than the Ramblers' Association. Its aims are clear: to foster a greater knowledge, love and care of the countryside; to assist in the protection and enhancement of public rights of way and areas of natural beauty; to work for greater public access to the countryside; and to encourage more people to take up rambling as a healthy, recreational leisure activity.

It was founded in 1935 when, following the setting up of a National Council of Ramblers' Federation in 1931, a number of federations in London, Manchester, the Midlands and elsewhere came together to create a more effective pressure group, to deal with such problems as the disappearance or obstruction of footpaths, the prevention of access to open mountain and moorland, and increasing hostility from landowners. This was the era of the mass trespasses, when there were sometimes violent confrontations between ramblers and gamekeepers, especially on the moorlands of the Peak District.

Since then the Ramblers' Association

has played a key role in preserving and developing the national footpath network, supporting the creation of national parks and encouraging the designation and waymarking of long-distance routes.

Our freedom of access to the countryside, now enshrined in legislation, is still in its early years and requires constant vigilance. But over and above this there will always be the problem of footpaths being illegally obstructed, disappearing through lack of use, or being extinguished by housing or road construction.

It is to meet such problems and dangers that the Ramblers' Association exists and represents the interests of all walkers. The address to write to for information on the Ramblers' Association and how to become a member is given on page 95.

 ### Walkers and the Law

TThe *Countryside and Rights of Way Act 2000 (CRoW)* extends the rights of access previously enjoyed by walkers in England and Wales. Implementation of these rights began on 19 September 2004. The Act amends existing legislation and for the first time provides access on foot to certain types of land – defined as mountain, moor, heath, down and registered common land.

Where You Can Go
Rights of Way
Prior to the introduction of *CRoW* walkers could only legally access the countryside along public rights of way. These are either 'footpaths' (for walkers only) or 'bridleways' (for walkers, riders on horseback and pedal cyclists). A third category called 'Byways open to all traffic' (BOATs), is used by motorised vehicles as well as those using non-mechanised transport. Mainly they are green lanes, farm and estate roads, although occasionally they will be found crossing mountainous area.

Rights of way are marked on Ordnance Survey maps. Look for the green broken lines on the Explorer maps, or the red dashed lines on Landranger maps.

The term 'right of way' means exactly what it says. It gives a right of passage over what, for the most part, is private land. Under pre-CRoW legislation walkers were required to keep to the line of the right of way and not stray onto land on either side. If you did inadvertently wander off the right of way, either because of faulty map reading or because the route was not clearly indicated on the ground, you were technically trespassing.

Local authorities have a legal obligation to ensure that rights of way are kept clear and free of obstruction, and are signposted where they leave metalled roads. The duty of local authorities to install signposts extends to the placing of signs along a path or way, but only where the authority considers it necessary to have a signpost or waymark to assist persons unfamiliar with the locality.

The New Access Rights
Access Land
As well as being able to walk on existing rights of way, under the new legislation you now have access to large areas of open land. You can of course continue to use rights of way footpaths to cross this land, but the main difference is that you can now lawfully leave the path and wander at will, but only in areas designated as access land.

Where to Walk
Areas now covered by the new access rights – Access Land – are shown on Ordnance Survey Explorer maps bearing the access land symbol on the front cover.

'Access Land' is shown on Ordnance Survey maps by a light yellow tint surrounded by a pale orange border. New orange coloured 'i' symbols on the maps will show the location of permanent access information boards installed by the access authorities.

Restrictions
The right to walk on access land may lawfully be restricted by landowners. Landowners can, for any reason, restrict

Countryside Access Charter

Your rights of way are:

- public footpaths – on foot only. Sometimes waymarked in yellow
- bridleways – on foot, horseback and pedal cycle. Sometimes waymarked in blue
- byways (usually old roads), most 'roads used as public paths' and, of course, public roads – all traffic has the right of way

Use maps, signs and waymarks to check rights of way. Ordnance Survey Explorer and Landranger maps show most public rights of way

On rights of way you can:

- take a pram, pushchair or wheelchair if practicable
- take a dog (on a lead or under close control)
- take a short route round an illegal obstruction or remove it sufficiently to get past

You have a right to go for recreation to:

- public parks and open spaces – on foot
- most commons near older towns and cities – on foot and sometimes on horseback
- private land where the owner has a formal agreement with the local authority

In addition you can use the following by local or established custom or consent, but ask for advice if you are unsure:

- many areas of open country, such as moorland, fell and coastal areas, especially those in the care of the National Trust, and some commons
- some woods and forests, especially those owned by the Forestry Commission
- country parks and picnic sites
- most beaches
- canal towpaths
- some private paths and tracks Consent sometimes extends to horse-riding and cycling

For your information:

- county councils and London boroughs maintain and record rights of way, and register commons
- obstructions, dangerous animals, harassment and misleading signs on rights of way are illegal and you should report them to the county council
- paths across fields can be ploughed, but must normally be reinstated within two weeks
- landowners can require you to leave land to which you have no right of access
- motor vehicles are normally permitted only on roads, byways and some 'roads used as public paths'

---

access for up to 28 days in any year. They cannot however close the land:

- on bank holidays;
- for more than four Saturdays and Sundays in a year;
- on any Saturday from 1 June to 11 August; or
- on any Sunday from 1 June to the end of September.

They have to provide local authorities with five working days' notice before the date of closure unless the land involved is an area of less than five hectares or the closure is for less than four hours. In these cases landowners only need to provide two hours' notice.

Whatever restrictions are put into place on access land they have no effect on existing rights of way, and you can continue to walk on them.

Dogs

Dogs can be taken on access land, but must be kept on leads of two metres or less between 1 March and 31 July, and at all times where they are near livestock. In addition landowners may impose a ban on all dogs from fields where lambing takes place for up to six weeks in any year. Dogs may be banned from moorland used for grouse shooting and breeding for up to five years.

In the main, walkers following the routes in this book will continue to follow existing rights of way, but a knowledge and understanding of the law as it affects walkers, plus the ability to distinguish access land marked on the maps, will enable anyone who wishes to depart from paths that cross access land either to take a shortcut, to enjoy a view or to explore.

General Obstructions

Obstructions can sometimes cause a problem on a walk and the most common of these is where the path across a field has been ploughed over. It is legal for a farmer to plough up a path provided that it is restored within two weeks. This does not always happen and you are faced with the dilemma of following the line of the path, even if this means treading on crops, or walking round the edge of the field. Although the later course of action seems the most sensible, it does mean that you would be trespassing.

Other obstructions can vary from overhanging vegetation to wire fences across the path, locked gates or even a cattle feeder on the path.

Use common sense. If you can get round the obstruction without causing damage, do so. Otherwise only remove as much of the obstruction as is necessary to secure passage.

If the right of way is blocked and cannot be followed, there is a long-standing view that in such circumstances there is a right to deviate, but this cannot wholly be relied on. Although it is accepted in law that highways (and that includes rights of way) are for the public service, and if the usual track is impassable, it is for the general good that people should be entitled to pass into another line. However, this should not be taken as indicating a right to deviate whenever a way becomes impassable. If in doubt, retreat.

Report obstructions to the local authority and/or the Ramblers' Association.

Global Positioning System (GPS)

What is GPS?

GPS is a worldwide radio navigation system that uses a network of 24 satellites and receivers, usually hand-held, to calculate positions. By measuring the time it takes a signal to reach the receiver, the distance from the satellite can be estimated. Repeat this with several satellites and the receiver can then use triangulation to establish the position of the receiver.

How to use GPS with Ordnance Survey mapping

Each of the walks in this book includes GPS co-ordinate data that reflects the walk position points on Ordnance Survey maps.

GPS and OS maps use different models for the earth and co-ordinate systems, so when you are trying to relate your GPS position to features on the map the two will differ slightly. This is especially the case with height, as the model that relates the GPS global co-ordinate system to height above sea level is very poor.

When using GPS with OS mapping, some distortion – up to 16ft (5m) – will always be present. Moreover, individual features on maps may have been surveyed only to an accuracy of 23ft (7m) (for 1:25000 scale maps), while other features, e.g. boulders, are usually only shown schematically.

In practice, this should not cause undue difficulty, as you will be near enough to your objective to be able to spot it.

How to use the GPS data in this book

There are various ways you can use the GPS data in this book.

1. Follow the route description while checking your position on your receiver when you are approaching a position point.

2. You can also use the positioning information on your receiver to verify where you are on the map.

3. Alternatively, you can use some of the proprietary software that is available. At the simple end there is inexpensive software, which lets you input the walk positions (waypoints), download them to the gps unit and then use them to assist your navigation on the walks.

Further Information

At the upper end of the market Ordnance Survey maps are available in electronic form. Most come with software that enables you to enter your walking route onto the map, download it to your gps unit and use it, alongside the route description, to follow the route.

 ## *Walking Safety*

Although the reasonably gentle country-side that is the subject of this book offers no real dangers to walkers at any time of the year, it is still advisable to take sensible precautions and follow certain well-tried guidelines.

Always take with you both warm and waterproof clothing and sufficient food and drink. Wear suitable footwear, such as strong walking boots or shoes that give a good grip over stony ground, on slippery slopes and in muddy conditions. Try to obtain a local weather forecast and bear it in mind before you start. Do not be afraid to abandon your proposed route and return to your starting point in the event of a sudden and unexpected deterioration in the weather.

All the walks described in this book will be safe to do, given due care and respect, even during the winter. Indeed, a crisp, fine winter day often provides perfect walking conditions, with firm ground underfoot and a clarity unique to this time of the year.

The most difficult hazard likely to be encountered is mud, especially when walking along woodland and field paths, farm tracks and bridleways – the latter in particular can often get churned up by cyclists and horses. In summer, an additional difficulty may be narrow and overgrown paths, particularly along the edges of cultivated fields. Neither should constitute a major problem provided that the appropriate footwear is worn.

 ## *The Cotswold Voluntary Warden Service*

The Cotswold Voluntary Warden Service was formed in 1968 in order to assist in the preservation and promotion of the Cotswolds Area of Outstanding Natural Beauty.

The principal objectives of the Warden Service are: to provide facilities which improve public access and enjoyment of the countryside; to promote the qualities of the countryside, thereby enhancing the public's appreciation of them; and to protect the countryside from excessive, potentially damaging use.

The service is administered by Cotswold County Council. Further information can be obtained from:

Cotswold Conservation Board,
Fosse Way, Northleach,
Gloucestershire
GL54 3JH.
Tel. 01451 862000

 ## *Useful Organisations*

Campaign to Protect Rural England
128 Southwark Street,
London SE1 0SW
Tel. 020 7981 2800
www.cpre.org.uk

Cotswold District Council
www.cotswold.gov.uk/go/tourism

Forestry Commission
Bank House, Bank Street,
Coleford, Gloucestershire
GL16 8BA
Tel. 01594 833057
www.forestry.gov.uk

Long Distance Walkers' Association
www.ldwa.org.uk

National Trust
Membership and general enquiries:
PO Box 39, Warrington,
WA5 7WD
Tel. 0870 458 4000
www.thenationaltrust.org.uk

Natural England
John Dower House, Crescent Place,
Cheltenham, Gloucestershire
GL50 3RA
Tel. 0300 060 2481
www.naturalengland.org.uk

Ordnance Survey
Romsey Road, Maybush,
Southampton
SO16 4GU
Tel. 08456 05 05 05 (Lo-call)
www.ordnancesurvey.co.uk

Ramblers' Association
2nd Floor, Camelford House,
87-90 Albert Embankment,
London SE1 7TW
Tel. 020 7339 8500
www.ramblers.org.uk

South West Tourism
Woodwater Park, Pynes Hill,
Rydon Lane, Exeter
EX2 5WT
Tel. 0870 442 0830
www.swtourism.co.uk

Local tourist information offices (*not
open all year):
Abingdon: 01235 522711
Banbury: 01295 259855
Bath: 0906 7112000
Burford: 01993 823558
Cheltenham: 01242 522878
Chippenham: 01249 706333
Chipping Norton: 01608 644379
Cirencester: 01285 654180
Evesham: 01386 446944
Gloucester: 01452 396572
*Northleach: 01451 860715
Stow-on-the-Wold: 01451 831082
Stroud: 01453 760960
Tetbury: 01666 503552
Tewkesbury: 01684 295027
*Winchcombe: 01242 602925
Witney: 01993 775802
Woodstock: 01993 813276

Youth Hostels Association
Trevelyan House, Dimple Road,
Matlock, Derbyshire, DE4 3YH

Tel. 01629 592600
www.yha.org.uk

 *Ordnance Survey maps
of the Cotswolds*
The area of *More Cotswold Walks* is
covered by Ordnance Survey 1:50 000
(1¼ inches to 1 mile or 2cm to 1km) scale
Landranger map sheets 150, 151, 162,
163, 164, 172, 173. These all-purpose
maps are packed with information to help
you explore the area. Viewpoints, picnic
sites, places of interest, caravan and
camping sites are shown, as well as public
rights of way information such as
footpaths and bridleways.

To examine the Cotswolds in more
detail and especially if you are planning
walks, Ordnance Survey Explorer maps at
1:25 000 (2½ inches to 1 mile or 4cm to
1km) scale are ideal:

155 Bristol & Bath
156 Chippenham & Bradford-on-Avon
157 Marlborough & Savernake Forest
158 Newbury & Hungerford
167 Thornbury, Dursley & Yate
168 Stroud, Tetbury & Malmesbury
169 Cirencester & Swindon
170 Abingdon, Wantage & Vale of White
     Horse
179 Gloucester, Cheltenham & Stroud
180 Oxford
191 Banbury, Bicester & Chipping Norton

Also at 1:25 000 scale (2½ inches to 1 mile
or 4cm to 1km) Explorer OL maps are
invaluable for walkers:

OL14 Wye Valley & Forest of Dean
OL45 The Cotswolds

To get to the Cotswolds use the Ordnance
Survey OS Travel-Map Route Great Britain
at 1:625 000 (1 inch to 10 miles or 4cm to
25 km) scale.

For touring, the OS Travel-Map Tour 8
(The Cotswolds & Gloucestershire) at a
scale of 1:100 000 (1cm to 1km or 1 inch
to 1½ miles) is ideal.

Ordnance Survey maps and guides
are available from most booksellers,
stationers and newsagents.

Further Information